OUT of TOUCH

OUT of TOUCH

The ELITE ONE PERCENT *and* *the* BATTLE *for* AMERICA'S SOUL

SCOTT W. RASMUSSEN

A REPUBLIC BOOK
ISBN: 978-1-64572-116-1
ISBN (eBook): 978-1-64572-117-8

Out of Touch:
The Elite One Percent and the Battle for America's Soul

Cover Design by Cody Corcoran

Republic Book Publishers
New York, NY
www.republicbookpublishers.com

Published in the United States of America
1 2 3 4 5 6 7 8 9 10

This book is dedicated to America's 519,000 state and local elected officials, who serve as the backbone of a self-governing society.

Table of Contents

Foreword

by Chris Rufo

Every political era tells itself a story about who holds power and why. In our own time, the prevailing story insists that America remains governed primarily through national elections, elite expertise, and centralized institutions acting in the public interest. Scott Rasmussen's *Out of Touch: The Elite One Percent and the Battle for America's Soul* challenges that story—and replaces it with a more honest, and ultimately more hopeful, account of how power actually functions in modern America.

The central claim of this book is straightforward but unsettling: a narrow elite has grown increasingly disconnected from the American people, while consolidating influence inside the institutions that shape culture, law, and daily life. This elite does not rule by popular consent so much as by insulation—buffered from voters, shielded from accountability, and confident in its moral authority. What Rasmussen calls the "Elite One Percent" is not defined merely by wealth, but by educational certification and urban access to narrative setting institutions. They occupy the commanding heights of media, education, bureaucracy, and corporate governance, and they increasingly see themselves as managers of society rather than servants of a self-governing people.

Much of today's political frustration stems from this divide. Americans are told they are polarized, misinformed, or resistant to progress. Yet Rasmussen's research consistently shows something strikingly different. Despite relentless cultural pressure and institutional disdain, the American people still overwhelmingly affirm the nation's founding ideals of freedom, equality, and self-governance. The problem is not that Americans have abandoned these principles. The problem is that many of the institutions meant to uphold them have been captured by elitists who reject those ideals.

This is where *Out of Touch* departs from the cynicism that often characterizes critiques of elite power. Rasmussen is not a declinist. He is an optimist—clear-eyed about dysfunction, but confident about the character of the American people. He believes, based on decades of research, that the moral core of the nation remains intact. The battle for America's soul is not a struggle to invent new values, but to reclaim old ones that still resonate deeply across class, race, and geography.

To understand why this reclamation is necessary, Rasmussen directs our attention away from the spectacle of national politics and toward the quieter machinery of institutional control. Elections still matter, but they increasingly operate within boundaries set by unelected actors: administrators who write rules, educators who shape worldviews, media professionals who frame legitimacy, and corporate managers who enforce ideological conformity. These institutions are not neutral. They encode values, reward certain behaviors, and marginalize others. When they drift ideologically, democracy itself begins to hollow out.

This institutional drift explains a defining paradox of our era: Voters sense that something is wrong, yet struggle to correct it through conventional political means. Policies change at the margins, while the underlying assumptions of governance remain fixed. Dissent is tolerated only so long as it does not threaten elite consensus. When it does, it is dismissed as dangerous, uninformed, or illegitimate. Rasmussen's great service is to name this dynamic plainly, without resorting to caricature or conspiracy.

Education plays a central role in this story. Schools and universities are not merely sites of instruction; they are engines of elite formation. When these institutions adopt ideological frameworks that divide society into permanent categories of oppressors and oppressed, they do more than promote a theory—they cultivate a ruling class mindset. Students trained in this way are taught not to persuade fellow citizens, but to manage them. Democracy becomes conditional, acceptable only when it produces the "right" outcomes.

Yet Rasmussen refuses to conclude that institutional capture is irreversible. On the contrary, *Out of Touch* advances a solution rooted deeply in American history and constitutional design: the revival of local self-governance. Long before power was centralized in Washington, America relied on a vast network of state and local officials—more than 519,000 of them today—to serve as the backbone of a self-governing society. These officials are closer to the people, more responsive to local concerns, and better positioned to reflect the values of their communities than distant bureaucracies ever could be.

This localist vision is not nostalgia. It is realism. Power gravitates toward institutions that are allowed to exercise it. For too long, Americans have ceded authority upward—trusting national experts to solve problems better handled closer to home. The result has been not efficiency, but alienation. Rasmussen argues persuasively that restoring balance requires empowering governors, state legislators, mayors, school boards, county commissioners, and other local leaders to reclaim their rightful role in shaping public life.

Crucially, this is not a call for chaos or fragmentation. It is a call for accountability. Local officials cannot hide behind abstraction. They live among the people they serve. They send their children to local schools. They answer to neighbors, not just national advocacy groups or federal agencies. In a healthy republic, this proximity is a strength. It grounds power in lived experience and shared responsibility.

Rasmussen's optimism flows directly from this insight. The American people are not waiting for salvation from elite institutions.

They are looking for practical steps to take—and encouragement—to govern themselves again. When given genuine authority, local leaders can counterbalance elite dominance and re-anchor institutions in the values of the communities they serve. This, Rasmussen suggests, is how democratic renewal actually happens: not through sweeping national reforms alone, but through steady, principled action across thousands of local jurisdictions.

Some critics will argue that this approach underestimates the complexity of modern governance. Rasmussen anticipates this objection and answers it implicitly: complexity is often the excuse of centralized power. Local governance does not reject expertise; it situates it within democratic control. Experts advise. Citizens decide. Institutions serve, rather than rule.

What makes *Out of Touch* especially compelling is its refusal to indulge despair. Rasmussen does not portray elites as omnipotent or the public as helpless. He insists instead on a harder truth: self-governance is demanding and every American has a role to play. It requires citizens to participate, local leaders to lead, and institutions to accept limits. But it is precisely this effort that gives democracy its dignity.

At stake is more than policy preference. At stake is whether America remains a nation where our government derives its legitimate authority from the consent or whether we will be ruled by out of touch elitists who believe they are destined to rule over the rest of us. Rasmussen's research suggests that a positive answer is still within reach. The values endure. The institutions can be reformed. The officials already exist. What is required is to bring decision making closer to home so that the American people can decide for themselves how to live their own lives.

This book will challenge readers across the political spectrum. It questions comfortable assumptions about expertise, progress, and centralized authority. But it does so in service of something constructive: a renewed confidence in the American people and the system of self-governance they inherited.

Out of Touch is ultimately a book about recovery—of memory, of responsibility, and of democratic agency. It reminds us that America's best days are not behind us because its founding ideals are not exhausted. They live on in the convictions of ordinary citizens and in the vast, often-overlooked network of local leaders capable of putting those convictions into practice.

The battle for America's soul will not be won by elites speaking for the people. It will be won by the people governing themselves. Scott Rasmussen shows us how—and why that work remains not only possible, but necessary.

Chapter 1

THE RIDDLE OF PARTISAN POLARIZATION

Many Americans today believe the nation's survival hinges on the next election. Their preferred candidate, they fear, is the only one who can protect them from the supposed dangers of the opposition. Others believe it's already too late—that the country is lost and all we can do now is grieve and manage the decline.

In this environment, I often begin public talks with a confession: I'm an optimist. I believe America's best days lie ahead. My children, and future generations, will live better lives than we can imagine. That outlook doesn't depend on who occupies the White House. I've voted in thirteen presidential elections since 1976, and most of my candidates lost. Yet my optimism has endured—through the administrations of Barack Obama, Donald Trump, and Joe Biden.

It's all a matter of perspective.

Many years ago, my wife, our young sons, and I joined a church service project to unload an eighteen-wheeler full of yams. Our task was to separate the good ones—those that could feed hungry children—from the rotten ones. After several hours in the heat of a North Carolina summer, we had barely made a dent. It was demoralizing.

Then someone turned around and looked the other way—toward the growing pile of good yams we had already sorted. The rest of us followed. That simple shift in perspective changed everything. What had felt futile became hopeful. We could see our impact, and it gave us energy to keep going.

Years later, as my confidence in the political system collapsed, I took a similar approach. I turned away from Washington and began looking at the rest of America. What I saw was hopeful: ordinary people solving problems in their communities. Each time I looked at America, rather than at American politics, my outlook improved.

That optimism doesn't come from feel-good stories alone. I see as much public-opinion polling data as anyone, and the numbers give me deep confidence in the American people. I am optimistic about America's future because I know that Americans still embrace our founding ideals of freedom, equality, and self-governance.

As a student of history, I also know that the views and values of the American people matter more than political dysfunction. Despite what we hear in the news, change in America almost always begins outside official Washington. That's how women won the right to vote, how Black Americans overcame Jim Crow, and even how 401(k) plans were created.

Still, while I'm optimistic, I don't believe a bright future is inevitable. Despite my confidence in the American people, I recognize that the hyper-partisanship of our broken political system poses a threat that could drag the nation down.

As *The Liberal Patriot*'s John Halpin put it, "Few, if any, elected officials inside the two political parties really care much about finding common ground." Rather than solving problems, he wrote,

"The politicians mostly like the current system—and perhaps profit from it."[1]

We have a lot of work to do.

America's partisan divide has become so deep that if Democrats declared water was wet, Republicans would argue the point. And if Republicans said the sky was blue, Democrats would beg to differ.

The Pew Research Center reports that just 9 percent of Republicans believe the Democratic Party governs in an honest and ethical way—and only 12 percent of Democrats say the same about the GOP. Most partisans view members of the opposing party as more dishonest than the average American. Majorities on both sides see the other team as less moral and more closed-minded.[2]

No wonder so many partisans believe every election will decide the fate of the nation.

My own polling found that just 41 percent of Republicans believe most Democrats love their country. And the mirror image is true: only 46 percent of Democrats believe most Republicans do.[3] Think about that. Most political partisans don't even believe the other side loves America. That's not a disagreement over policy; it's something close to accusing the other side of treason.

This mindset infects not only voters but also political leaders. James Carville, the legendary Democratic strategist, once said he was "not convinced at all that Donald Trump loves the United

---

1 John Halpin, "Citizenship Without Partisanship," *The Liberal Patriot*, September 14, 2023, https://www.liberalpatriot.com/p/citizenship-without-partisanship.

2 "Partisan Hostility Grows Alongside a Desire for Compromise," Pew Research Center, August 9, 2022, https://www.pewresearch.org/politics/2022/08/09/as-partisan-hostility-grows-signs-of-frustration-with-the-two-party-system/.

3 September 24–25, 2024—Napolitan Institute data from survey of 1,000 registered voters.

States."[4] President Trump, for his part, said Democrats "don't love our country."[5]

This kind of mutual disdain fuels demonization, not dialogue. It tears the country apart and blocks the path to solving shared problems. Unfortunately, it plays out not only in Washington but also in everyday communities across the nation.

Two women I know have been friends for nearly fifty years. They grew up together in the Midwest, went to school together, married in the same year, and became mothers around the same time. Though life eventually took them to different parts of the country, they stayed in touch. Their shared values and long history built a bond that once seemed unshakable.

But today there's one subject they dare not discuss: politics. Even something as small as a comment on social media feels risky. They fear it could explode and damage the friendship they've spent a lifetime building.

What's striking is that neither woman is particularly political. They're not activists. In fact, their values—and their common-sense view of politics—are remarkably similar. Yet modern politics has built a wall between them that even decades of friendship can't climb over.

This is no longer unusual; it's the new normal. Just 21 percent of voters say they can talk politics with a friend from the other side. A slightly larger share—25 percent—say they've lost friendships over political differences.[6]

---

4 Ben Blanchet, "'No Bigger Crisis': James Carville Nails the 'Profound' Problem with Trump's Return," *HuffPost*, March 14, 2025, https://www.huffpost.com/entry/james-carville-donald-trump-no-bigger-crisis-america_n_67d3bf9de4b0e72dd7ff2295.

5 Donald Trump (@realDonaldTrump), "The Democrats are all "giddy" about…" Truth Social, January 3, 2025, 1:31 PM, https://truthsocial.com/@realDonaldTrump/posts/113765847370756395.

6 March 6, 2025— Napolitan News data from survey of 1,000 registered voters.

Even those numbers fail to convey the depth of America's political divide. Incredibly, Americans today are more likely to have friends of a different race than of a different political party. More people would rather live in a racially mixed community than in one with political diversity.[7]

Having grown up during the civil rights era, I still find it hard to believe that America's partisan divide now runs deeper than our racial or ethnic divides. When I was a child, Black Americans in the South couldn't sit at the same lunch counters as White Americans. I'm thankful for how far we've come on race—but deeply troubled that today's divisions have shifted to partisan politics and become just as corrosive.

For the future of our country, we must reverse that trend. It's dangerous that so many Americans now prefer to live in communities where they don't hear opposing views. If we never engage with people who think differently, how can we possibly understand them—or find common ground?

I recognize that many Americans have little interest in that kind of understanding. That's a shame, because even a modest effort would reveal that America isn't nearly as polarized in everyday life as it is in politics. Like the two Midwestern friends I mentioned earlier, most people share more values than they realize. But politics makes those shared values harder to see.

As we approach our nation's 250th birthday, 70 percent of voters still believe that government derives its only legitimate authority from the consent of the governed. Eighty-five percent believe that we are all created equal and endowed by our Creator with the inalienable right to life, liberty, and the pursuit of happiness. Voters from

---

7 September 18–19, 2024— Napolitan News data from survey of 1,000 registered voters.

both parties affirm those ideals—but they don't believe the other side does.[8]

In a world shaped by toxic partisanship, that mistrust becomes self-reinforcing. Outreach across party lines grows rare. Americans increasingly assume that members of the opposing party are more closed-minded, less moral, even unpatriotic. In that context, the desire for politically pure communities makes a troubling kind of sense. After all, nobody wants to live next to someone who hates America.

How did we get to this point?

For many Americans, the answer is simple: Donald Trump.

According to CNN's John King, "Trump divided America as a candidate. So far, he's doing the same as president."[9] *The Guardian* quoted an Ohio woman who said her family is "totally divided" because of Trump. "Some of us are no longer speaking with each other," she said. The same article claimed that "millions of families" face similar problems.[10]

It's easy to understand why these beliefs are so widespread. Donald Trump is an extraordinarily polarizing figure who provokes intense reactions—both positive and negative. Some view him as a national savior; others see him as a threat to democracy. He has dominated the political landscape for the past decade and may prove to be the most consequential president since Ronald Reagan.

But the fact that so many blame Trump for the current toxicity in American politics doesn't necessarily make it true.

---

[8] June 25–26, 2025— Napolitan News data from survey of 1,000 registered voters.

[9] John King, "Trump divided America as a candidate. So far, he's doing the same as president," CNN, January 27, 2025, https://www.cnn.com/2025/01/26/politics/voter-reaction-trump-first-week-aotm/index.html.

[10] Jem Bartholomew, "'It's so crushing': US families navigate divide over politics during the holidays," *The Guardian,* December 23, 2024, https://www.theguardian.com/us-news/2024/dec/23/family-politics-holiday.

In fact, the numbers tell a different story: America's political divide didn't begin with Donald Trump. It started long before he entered the political arena.

One simple measure of that divide is the partisan gap in presidential job approval. Today, Republicans automatically disapprove of a Democratic president, and Democrats automatically disapprove of a Republican one.

In March 2025, for instance, 90 percent of Republicans approved of the way President Trump was doing his job. Just 18 percent of Democrats agreed—a 72-point partisan approval gap.[11]

It's hard for Americans today to imagine anything else. Of course Democrats disapprove of a Republican president. Why wouldn't they?

But that kind of partisan reflex is a relatively recent phenomenon. In March 1965, a majority of Republicans (57 percent) approved of newly inaugurated Democrat Lyndon Johnson. Four years later, most Democrats (55 percent) gave Republican President Richard Nixon a thumbs-up. And in March 1977, 60 percent of Republicans approved of Democrat Jimmy Carter.

Those early-term snapshots show that Americans once routinely rallied around a new president, regardless of party, and hoped for his success. That spirit has vanished in the twenty-first century.[12]

The goodwill didn't last. Each of those presidents left office deeply unpopular. But even their declining support shows how much things have changed. Johnson's approval among Democrats dipped to 48 percent. Nixon's approval among Republicans fell to the same level. Carter's sank even lower, with just 34 percent of Democrats approving by the end.[13]

---

11 "Presidential Job Approval Center," Gallup, accessed December 3, 2025, https://news.gallup.com/interactives/507569/presidential-job-approval-center.aspx.

12 Ibid.

13 Ibid.

You don't see that today. Throughout his presidency, Joe Biden's approval among Democrats never dropped below 75 percent. In his first term, Donald Trump's numbers among Republicans never fell below 79 percent.[14]

That's not loyalty; it's partisanship on autopilot. It's like believing your football team is winning, no matter how badly they're actually playing.

In earlier decades, partisanship mattered—but it wasn't everything. Americans were willing to criticize a president from their own party. They could even give credit to one from the other side when it was deserved.

That's not how it works in America today.

It's important to note that the rise of partisan polarization didn't happen overnight. It crept in gradually—president by president, over four decades.

When George H. W. Bush took office in 1989, the partisan approval gap was 35 points (78 percent of Republicans approved, versus 43 percent of Democrats). By the time Bill Clinton was elected in 1992, the gap had widened to 53 points. George W. Bush started his term with a 56-point divide, which grew to 64 under Barack Obama.

For those who think Trump broke American politics, it's worth remembering that Obama's first major legislative victory—the 2009 stimulus package—received zero Republican votes in the House. The public reaction to Obama's highly partisan approach helped spark sweeping GOP victories in the 2010 midterms and set the tone for a deeply divided decade.

Trump entered office with a 77-point partisan approval gap. But Joe Biden topped even that—just two months into his presidency, the gap had soared to 86 points.

---

14 Ibid.

These numbers make one thing clear: The Trump era didn't create polarization. It accelerated a trend that was already decades in the making.

But that's not how it feels to the two Midwestern women. For them, Donald Trump remains a political third rail. One is deeply opposed to him and the MAGA movement; the other supports many of his policies but is often disappointed—or offended—by his behavior. To preserve their friendship, they've learned not to say his name.

And they're not alone. Millions of Americans believe the Trump era marks a rupture from everything that came before. The idea that Trump is part of a longer political trend—just another chapter in the partisan story—strikes many on both sides as absurd.

As *The New York Times* columnist Ezra Klein put it, Democrats viewed Trump's 2016 victory as "an aberration that must be explained." "Reality," he wrote, "had ruptured. We were owed answers."[15]

Many Trump supporters shared the belief that something extraordinary had happened—but they reached the opposite conclusion: "Donald J. Trump Saved America from Hillary Clinton."[16]

That belief only deepened in the years that followed. The 2020 and 2024 elections, along with the near-miss assassination attempt against Trump, added a mythic dimension to the story, turning him into a figure whose rise and survival seemed beyond politics as usual.

But once again, that's not what the data show.

Historically, the numbers suggest something very different: Donald Trump didn't cause America's political divide—he's a product of it.

---

15 Ezra Klein, *Why We're Polarized* (Avid Reader Press: 2020, updated 2021), ix.

16 Howie Carr, *What Really Happened: How Donald J. Trump Saved America from Hillary Clinton* (Frandel: 2018).

Beginning in 1988—right around the time the partisan approval gap began to widen—America entered a new era of electoral deadlock. For the first time in US history, we've gone more than forty years without a presidential landslide.

It's unprecedented.[17]

- In the past ten presidential elections, not a single candidate has won the popular vote by double digits.
- In the ten elections before that (1948–1984), six resulted in landslides.
- And in the ten before that (1908–1944), there were seven landslides.

Why does this matter?

Because landslides play a vital role in democratic life. They cleanse the political system, bestow legitimacy on the winners, and force losing parties to reassess. Without landslides, polarization calcifies.

The last true landslide came in 1984, when Ronald Reagan beat Walter Mondale by 18 points and carried forty-nine states. He came within 4,000 votes of winning all fifty.[18] It's nearly impossible to imagine such an outcome today.

Reagan's sweeping victory left no doubt. No one claimed Mondale might have won if he'd tweaked his ads or visited a few more swing states. Democrats didn't spin the results. They absorbed the loss, realized that promising to raise taxes was a political non-starter, and adjusted.

---

[17] The longest previous stretch was seven straight elections from 1876 to 1900. That was also a very divisive time in US history following the Civil War.

[18] All references to election results come from David Leip's Election Atlas. David Leip, "Atlas of U.S. Presidential Elections," accessed December 3, 2025, https://uselectionatlas.org.

Eight years later, a more centrist Democrat, Bill Clinton, won the White House.

Clinton's margins of victory were narrow: He was elected with just 43 percent of the popular vote in 1992 and was reelected in 1996 with less than 50 percent. The new president got the message and famously declared that "the era of big government is over."[19]

That's what landslides do. They break partisan illusions and force political movements to face reality.

However you slice it, something shifted in American politics around 1988. That year marked the beginning of an era of electoral stagnation. For those who still believe Donald Trump caused our national divide, the historical record tells a different story.

Consider this: Over the past forty years, the average margin of victory in the popular vote has been just 3.9 percentage points. Compare that to the twenty elections before 1988, when the average margin was 13.6 points—more than three times as large.

The same trend shows up in the Electoral College:

- Between 1908 and 1944, six of ten elections resulted in the winner taking 80 percent or more of the electoral votes.
- From 1948 to 1984, six more elections produced similar blowouts.
- But in the last ten elections, not one candidate has come close to that level of dominance.

To win 80 percent of the Electoral College today—431 out of 538 votes—is practically unthinkable.

The implication is clear: The political fracture began long before Trump. It predates his entry into politics. It even predates his time as

[19] William Jefferson Clinton, "State of the Union Address," Clinton White House Archives, January 23, 1996, https://clintonwhitehouse4.archives.gov/WH/New/other/sotu.html.

a reality TV star. The rise of extreme polarization was well underway before most Americans had ever heard his name.

In his book *Why We're Polarized*, Ezra Klein describes the unsettling realization he reached after poring over the data and discussing it with colleagues: Donald Trump's 2016 victory, shocking as it felt, was not a rupture but a continuation.

Yes, Trump the candidate was unlike Mitt Romney, John McCain, or George W. Bush. But the dynamics behind his 2016 win—demographic divides, partisan sorting, electoral polarization—were already well established. The changes were at the margins, not at the core.

As Klein examined the data, he uncovered an even more unsettling reality. Over the past forty years, as Americans have grown more partisan in their voting "we have come to like the party we vote for less."[20] People on both sides of the political divide have been disappointed by their elected politicians and governing failures.

If we like our own party even less, how have we become more partisan? Klein explained this apparent disconnect is caused by what political scientists call *negative partisanship*—an intense and growing dislike of the opposing party. In other words, while we're disappointed with our own political team, we have come to dislike or hate the other team even more.

That distinction matters.

If we're serious about fixing what's broken in American politics, we have to understand what's actually broken. We need to solve the riddle of polarization.

Why do two lifelong friends in the Midwest—women who share values, history, and community—feel like they're on opposite sides of a battlefield? Why can't they even say the name "Trump" aloud?

---

[20] Klein, 10.

If Donald Trump is not to blame—if he is not the cause of our great political divide—then we need to figure out who or what is responsible. Because polarization this deep doesn't happen by accident. Somewhere along the way, powerful incentives—and powerful people—pushed us in this direction. Understanding that is the first step toward finding our way back.

Chapter 2

THE ELITE ONE PERCENT

I conducted my first public-opinion survey in the late 1980s, just as the streak of ten close presidential elections was beginning. Since then, I've probably conducted more polls than anyone else on the planet. That experience gives me a unique perspective on this unsettling period in American history—and has set me on a long journey to understand the root cause of our destructive partisan polarization.

Back then, I was a pollster for the term-limits movement, leading a coalition of state-based groups seeking to impose limits on members of Congress. Term limits were among the most consistently popular political reforms in American history, enjoying 70 to 80 percent support decade after decade.

Yet media coverage often labeled the movement "controversial." Talk about fake news! How could an issue so widely supported be controversial? Voters across parties, regions, and demographics backed it. What were the reporters thinking?

At first, I assumed the problem was simple: a lack of awareness. I spent hours reviewing polling data with reporters and Washington officials, showing them how overwhelmingly popular term limits had become. I quickly learned it didn't matter. Voters' views were largely irrelevant to those in power.

Political insiders were open about their condescension. *Politico*, for example, portrayed the public itself as the obstacle. Alexander Burns, now a senior editor there, dismissed ordinary Americans as lacking "even the most basic grasp of...the national political debate" and criticized "the sheer irrationality and volatility of voters' views on most issues."[21]

This attitude is emblematic of what I call the *Political Class*. Tom Jensen of Public Policy Polling put it bluntly: "The first lesson you learn as a pollster is that people are stupid."[22] He tells his clients that "at least once a week." That dismissive mindset captures the divide between Washington elites and the rest of the country—a divide that has shaped the political dysfunction we see today.

It's impossible to overstate how much I disagree with Jensen. I share instead the view of legendary pollster Joe Napolitan: "You should never underestimate the intelligence of the American people nor overestimate the level of knowledge at their disposal."[23] Voters may not know the intricate games politicians play, but they understand something far more important—life beyond the political bubble.

Napolitan worked for John F. Kennedy, Lyndon B. Johnson, Hubert Humphrey, and many other national leaders of his era. He also went to high school with my best friend's father, a connection that led him to give me an hour of his time for free. Looking back, I wish I'd asked better questions—but even then, it was an extraordinary opportunity for a high school student. The perspective he shared is one I continue to embrace.

---

21 Alexander Burns, "How much do voters know?" *Politico*, March 13, 2012, https://www.politico.com/story/2012/03/are-voters-dumb-073947.

22 Ibid.

23 Napolitan Institute, accessed December 3, 2025, https://napolitaninstitute.org/.

That respect for the wisdom of voters has often put me at odds with the political world. While most insiders see voters as the problem, I see the Political Class as the problem—and voters as the solution.

During the Tea Party era, I experienced a striking example of Political Class arrogance. After a presentation I gave at Harvard, a clearly exasperated professor complained about the growing voter unrest and populist attitudes. She seemed genuinely troubled that ordinary Americans were demanding to be heard.

"Why won't the people just let us lead?" she asked. "It's what we were trained to do."

Wow. Why indeed should Harvard-trained officials be challenged by mere voters? Why should they be subject to checks and balances from people who might not even hold a college degree? For me, that comment crystallized years of polling data showing that those with postgraduate degrees often inhabit a very different world from the rest of America.

To be clear, I have immense respect for thoughtful scholars, rigorous research, and serious intellectual debate. I'm also not suggesting that every person with a postgraduate degree is disconnected from everyday Americans—full disclosure, I hold an MBA myself. But I do reject the notion that a degree, even from an elite institution, makes someone inherently superior to anyone else.

In response to the professor's question, I simply made what seemed like an obvious observation: "The voters don't like where you want to lead them."

Over time, however, I came to see that brief exchange as symbolic of the most important divide in American politics today:

- On one side are the vast majority of Americans who continue to embrace our founding ideals of freedom, equality, and self-governance.

- On the other is a small—but powerful—elitist minority that rejects those ideals and believes some people are destined to rule over others.

It's hard for me to wrap my head around, but apparently some people genuinely believe the rest of us would be better off simply doing what the elite "experts" tell us. That disconnect is visible in countless issues—like term limits—that enjoy broad popular support yet are ignored, dismissed, or labeled "controversial" by the *Political Class*. It's also reflected in the fact that 77 percent of voters believe the government doesn't pay enough attention to what the American people want.[24]

Having grown up believing that voters are supposed to be in charge, I was—and remain—deeply offended by this reality. That's not the way America is supposed to work.

The anger I felt over Political Class arrogance became the driving force of my polling career. I wanted to expose their views and behaviors. A couple of decades ago, I even created a *Political Class Index* to track just how wide the gap had grown between everyday Americans and their political "leaders."

The Index revealed some striking patterns. For example, it helped explain why the media often labeled term limits "controversial." While supporting term limits was a no-brainer for voters, the issue was deeply divisive among the Political Class itself—only 56 percent favored it, while 43 percent opposed.[25] National reporters ignored the voters and treated the Political Class's views as if they were the only ones that mattered.

---

[24] March 6-7, 2024, Napolitan Institute data from survey of 1,000 registered voters

[25] April 14–21, 2025—Napolitan News data from survey of 2,000 registered voters.

Looking back, that pattern of misleading coverage offers a window into the decline of legacy media over the past forty years. Political Class reporters rarely told stories from the perspective of ordinary Americans. Instead, they focused only on what official Washington deemed important. No wonder the American people gradually tuned them out.

As I dug deeper into the root causes of our partisan polarization, the *Political Class Index* proved both useful and revealing. It gave me a way to identify dozens of issues where Americans—like the two Midwestern women I mentioned earlier—agreed across party lines, often in ways that official Washington routinely rejected.

At the same time, the Index had its limits. For practical and cost reasons, it didn't measure the views of those actually shaping the political narrative. Instead, it captured the attitudes of ordinary voters who happened to share elite viewpoints on a handful of key issues. It was a reasonable proxy, but not a substitute for surveying the Political Class directly. I knew I needed a better approach.

As I reviewed thousands of polling interviews each week, I looked for clues to document what I saw as a growing threat to America's founding ideals. Over time, three groups consistently emerged as holding views sharply out of step with most voters:

- Voters with a postgraduate degree
- Voters living in densely populated urban areas (at least 10,000 people per square mile in their ZIP code)
- Voters earning $150,000 or more per year

Beyond being out of step with most voters, these three groups shared another trait: They were elite in ways that gave them real influence. Each had access to people, places, and opportunities far beyond the reach of everyday Americans. With their resources and connections, they could shape the political conversation in ways most citizens never could.

I theorized that those who combined all three attributes—advanced degrees, high incomes, and urban residence—were likely the most disconnected of all. A postgrad in Manhattan would see the world very differently from a postgrad in Cedar Rapids. Likewise, a postgrad earning less than $150,000 in a small town could hold attitudes very unlike someone pursuing a high-powered career on K Street.

To test the theory, I combined tens of thousands of survey interviews my firm had conducted. Only about 1 percent of voters have all three elite attributes, so I needed that many to get a clear picture. All the surveys asked one common question: Did voters approve or disapprove of President Joe Biden's performance? That one question was enough to reveal something striking.

Across the full sample, Biden's approval stood at 41 percent. Among the tiny group with all three elite traits, approval jumped to 82 percent. It was like discovering a Grand Canyon of political divides—the elites on one side, everyone else on the other.

I couldn't release the results yet—there were only a few hundred respondents in that elite category. But the numbers confirmed what I suspected: The divide was real, profound, and demanded a larger, more focused survey to fully understand.

It took some time and a bit of salesmanship, but I eventually persuaded the Committee to Unleash Prosperity (CTUP) to sponsor an initial survey of 1,000 members of what we came to call the Elite One Percent. The results were nothing short of astonishing.

Nearly half—47 percent—of the Elite One Percent said there is *too much individual freedom* in America. You read that right: too much freedom.[26] Who thinks that? Outside the political world, I can't recall ever hearing anyone express such a sentiment. For most Americans, most of the time, the complaint is the exact opposite: *too little* freedom.[27]

---

26 September 11-26, 2023— Napolitan Institute survey of 1,000 elites.

27 September 18019, 2023— Napolitan Institute survey of 1,000 registered voters.

For someone who had spent decades trying to understand the Political Class's resistance to the American people, the results were thrilling. But at the same time, for someone who believes that governments derive their only legitimate authority from the consent of the governed, the findings were deeply unsettling.

Does the Unites States Provide Too Much Individual Freedom, Too Much Government Control, or is the Balance About Right?			
	Voters	Elite One Percent	Politically Active Elites
Too Much Individual Freedom	16%	47%	69%
Too Much Government Control	57%	21%	12%
Balance About Right	21%	29%	18%

Voters, of course, saw things very differently. Only 16 percent agreed with the Elite One Percent that Americans enjoy too much freedom. In sharp contrast, a majority—57 percent—felt the country suffers from *too much government control.*[28]

As I reviewed the first round of data, one subset of the Elite One Percent stood out: those who talk politics every day, a group I call the *Politically Active Elites*. These are the people shaping headlines, framing debates, and driving the national narrative—and their views were even more extreme than their peers.

Chillingly, when asked whether the American people have too much individual freedom, 69 percent of the Politically Active Elites said yes.[29] The gap between everyday Americans and the nation's most influential elites could not have been clearer—or more unsettling.

In my search to understand why our political system was so badly broken, the *Elite One Percent* seemed like the natural place to start. Every survey we conducted revealed new ways this influential group was out of touch with the rest of America. Looking at the data, it was easy to see why a populist mood was sweeping the country.

---

[28] Ibid.

[29] Ibid.

The more I saw, the angrier I became. Being offended by the views and behavior of the Political Class wasn't just understandable—it was the only rational response for anyone who believed in America's founding ideals.

At the same time, I was wary of *"off with their heads"* populism. After all, George Washington and Thomas Jefferson were, by any definition, elites of their time—and both were essential in defining the ideals that made America exceptional. Unlike the founding elites, who sought to balance governance with liberty, today's Political Class often favors centralized solutions, even when voters disagree.

The Rev. Dr. Martin Luther King Jr., as a Black man born in 1929, would never have been considered part of America's elite. Yet by virtue of his education and leadership, he occupied the elite circles of Black America in his day. Without his moral authority, the Civil Rights Movement would never have succeeded.

Still, while recognizing that elites will always play a leadership role in our nation, we must also protect ourselves from elitists who disregard voters and impose their own agendas. This tension lies at the heart of the challenge of designing and maintaining legitimate government. As James Madison observed, "If men were angels, no government would be necessary. If angels were to govern men, neither external nor internal controls on government would be necessary."[30]

Today, as in Madison's time, neither everyday Americans nor the *Elite One Percent* are particularly angelic. We need government—and we need elites to play an important role. The question is how to build enough checks and balances so that our leaders serve the voters rather than pursuing ideological or self-serving agendas.

To answer that question in the twenty-first century, we must first understand the elitists themselves—and how they helped break our

[30] James Madison and Alexander Hamilton, "Federalist 51," 1788, https://constitutioncenter.org/the-constitution/historic-document-library/detail/james-madison-federalist-no-51-1788.

political system. A natural starting point: Why do so many of them believe the American people have *too much* individual freedom?

A partial answer emerged from one of the most striking findings in our early research: 70 percent of the *Elite One Percent* said they trust the federal government to do the right thing most of the time[31]—a level of faith that aligns closely with a liberal, technocratic worldview. In more than three decades of polling, I had never seen anything like it. To most voters, that level of trust is simply incomprehensible.

How could anyone be so trusting, given everything we've witnessed over the years? Among the general public, only about 20 percent typically trust the government to do the right thing most of the time.[32] Decades of missteps, scandals, and bureaucratic indifference have earned the American people every ounce of their skepticism.

Our research revealed an enormous trust gap: Seven out of ten members of the *Elite One Percent* trust the government, while eight out of ten everyday Americans do not. That divide explains much about the dynamics of contemporary American politics.

The connection to attitudes about individual freedom is equally clear. Voters who don't trust the government naturally want more freedom—after all, who wants to take orders from a distant, untrustworthy Capitol elite?

By contrast, elites who *do* trust the government tend to believe that we would all be better off following the rules written by their preferred experts. From their perspective, individual freedom is a troublesome and illogical threat to the orderly society they hope to impose. To paraphrase Darth Vader, these elitists find the voters' lack of faith disturbing.

---

31 September 11-26, 2023— Napolitan Institute survey of 1,000 elites.

32 "Public Trust in Government: 1958-2024," Pew Research Center, June 24, 2024, https://www.pewresearch.org/politics/2024/06/24/public-trust-in-government-1958-2024/.

Making matters worse, these elites are a bit delusional; they don't even realize the trust gap exists. Two-thirds of the *Elite One Percent*—65 percent—mistakenly believe that most Americans actually trust the federal government to do the right thing most of the time.[33]

This is one of those findings that makes me shake my head and wonder what planet they're living on. For as long as I can remember, kitchen-table conversations and popular culture alike have been filled with references to government corruption, incompetence, and the untrustworthiness of elected officials.

Not only that, but the Pew Research Center and other organizations have documented persistently deep levels of voter distrust year after year, decade after decade. How could a group of successful postgraduates fail to recognize this fundamental reality of American politics?

Their selective blindness to reality reminded me of an experiment conducted in the late 1990s by psychologists Christopher F. Chabris and Daniel Jones Simons. The professors created a video of two teams passing basketballs and asked study participants to count the number of passes made by the team wearing white. At the same time, they were to ignore the passes made by the team wearing black. Given all the movement and different types of passes, it required a fair amount of concentration.

In the middle of the one-minute video, a female student wearing a full-body gorilla suit walked into the scene, stopped in the middle of the players, and stayed on camera for about nine seconds. About half the participants were so focused on the task at hand—counting the number of passes—that they never saw the gorilla.[34]

I suspect that something similar is going on with the Elite One Percent. They are so busy watching for things that matter to elites

---

[33] September 11-26, 2023— Napolitan Institute survey of 1,500 elites.

[34] Christoper Chabris and Daniel Simons, *The Invisible Gorilla,* (New York: Random House, 2009), 5.

that they can't see what's right in front of them—the public's obvious distrust of politics, politicians, and government.

Whatever the reason, this elitist misunderstanding of the American people helped pave the way for Donald Trump's rise.

In August 2015, then-candidate Trump participated in his first presidential debate. At one point, Fox News moderator Bret Baier challenged him to explain past contributions to the likely Democratic nominee, Hillary Clinton. It sounded like a gotcha question—but Trump handled it like a softball and knocked it out of the park.

Trump stated his view plainly: "When you give, they do whatever the hell you want them to do."[35]

Then he elaborated: "I will tell you that our system is broken. I gave to many people. Before this—before two months ago—I was a businessman. I give to everybody. When they call, I give." He explained why: "When I need something from them two years later, three years later, I call them—they are there for me."[36]

Trump went a step further, driving the point home to some of his challengers: "Most of the people on this stage I've given to, just so you understand—a lot of money."[37]

That answer (and others like it during the debate) did more than rattle the Political Class. It helped Trump connect with voters in a way the elites couldn't. He understood the transactional nature of politics—and wasn't afraid to say it aloud.

Later that night, Frank Luntz's focus group reassured political insiders that "Trump lost vital support." *Politico*, the insider publication that often fretted about the "irrationality" of voters, collected reactions from twenty-three political experts. Almost all concluded,

---

35 "Transcript of the 2015 GOP Debate (9 pm)" CBS News, August 7, 2015, https://www.cbsnews.com/news/transcript-of-the-2015-gop-debate-9-pm/.
36 Ibid.
37 Ibid.

in one form or another, "Trump lost."[38] The elites were horrified by his candid acknowledgment of how Washington really works.

Voters, in contrast, saw something very different. They watched an unconventional candidate state plainly what everyone already knew to be true. Even Republicans who disliked Trump—and Democrats who disliked all Republicans—recognized the honesty and authenticity in his comments. After all, why else would a businessman give money to politicians?

Trump's unvarnished acknowledgment of a broken political system stood in sharp contrast to the other candidates, many of whom—reflecting elite liberal orthodoxy—pretended the system functioned smoothly. That contrast didn't just win him a debate moment. It helped secure the nomination and, ultimately, the presidency.

---

[38] Politico Magazine, "The Debate's Biggest Winners—And Losers," *Politico,* August 7, 2015, https://www.politico.com/magazine/story/2015/08/republican-debate-2015-winners-losers-121139/.

Chapter 3

REMEMBER WHO THE REAL ENEMY IS

Who are the people who believe the rest of us have too much freedom—yet can't understand why nearly half the country voted for Donald Trump?

The Elite One Percent hold postgraduate degrees, live in densely populated urban centers, and earn at least $150,000 a year. They are distinct from the wealthiest one percent of income earners, but their influence is enormous: They shape media narratives, academic research, corporate policy, and government agendas. Their priorities and worldview are often far removed from those of the broader population.

Their influence isn't accidental. As political scientist Thomas R. Dye observes, "Power is concentrated in large institutions: corporations, banks and investment firms, insurance companies, media empires, the White House, Congress and the Washington bureaucracy, prestigious law firms and powerful lobbyists, 'fat cat' political contributors, foundations, universities, and private policy-planning organizations."[39]

---

[39] Thomas R. Dye, *Who's Running America?* (Routledge: 2014, 8th edition).

Power, he notes, "is not just about individuals; it is an attribute of roles in a social system.... People are powerful when they occupy positions of authority and control in social organizations."[40] In short, the Elite One Percent operates through institutional leverage—not merely personal wealth or fame.

Many in this group advocate for policies that would radically restrict everyday choices: banning gas-powered cars and SUVs, limiting air travel to essential trips, regulating the use of gas stoves and private air conditioning, and severely curbing private gun ownership.[41]

Demographically, this elite population is predominantly male (68 percent), White (77 percent), and between thirty-five and fifty-four years old (67 percent).[42] But the most consequential feature of the Elite One Percent is not their age, gender, or race—it is how far their experiences and priorities diverge from those of ordinary Americans.

This group is not identical to the broader Political Class, though there is considerable overlap. Members of the Elite One Percent are far more likely than the average American to discuss politics regularly—and many political insiders are more concerned with winning approval from these elites than with securing the consent of the governed.

Unsurprisingly, only 9 percent of them would describe themselves as "elites." Most people instinctively equate elites with wealth, and many in the Elite One Percent are surrounded by individuals who have far more money. A young lawyer in Manhattan earning $150,000 is hardly among the city's economic elite, though she may be someday. It makes sense, then, that two-thirds of the group classify themselves as upper-middle or upper class rather than elite.

---

40 Ibid.

41 Napolitan Institute, "Elite 1 Percent", September 2024, p. 7

42 Ibid., p. 16

Even more striking, 21 percent consider themselves middle class, and 4 percent identify as working class.[43] Still, it is easy to see how a well-paid college professor might feel financially stretched in one of America's most expensive cities. Despite being far from the economic elite, that professor often occupies a central role in the political and cultural conversations that shape the nation. When he speaks, important people listen.

The Elite One Percent wields influence across nearly every major sector of American life. In media, they dominate networks such as ABC, CBS, NBC, Fox, and CNN, as well as leading newspapers including *The New York Times* and *The Washington Post*. In higher education, their reach extends through sixty-two private colleges with endowments exceeding one billion dollars each.[44]

Dye argues that civic and policy influence is concentrated in organizations such as the Council on Foreign Relations, Trilateral Commission, Committee on Economic Development, Business Roundtable, Brookings Institution, American Enterprise Institute, Heritage Foundation, and Center for American Progress. On the cultural side, elites shape taste and discourse through institutions like the Metropolitan Museum of Art, Museum of Modern Art, Smithsonian, and Lincoln Center for the Performing Arts.

These networks ensure that the Elite One Percent's worldview is not only amplified but normalized across American society, creating a feedback loop that reinforces their priorities and perspectives.

Dye notes that collectively, the top institutional positions these elites occupy "control over half the nation's industrial assets, over half of all US banking assets, and over three-quarters of all insurance assets. They control the television networks, the investment firms, the influential newspapers, and the major media conglomerates. They control over half of all the assets of private foundations and two-thirds of all

---

[43] March 6-12, 2024—Napolitan Institute data from survey of 500 elites.

[44] Dye, *Who's Running America?, p. 9*

private university endowments. They direct the nation's largest and best-known law firms in New York and Washington, as well as the nation's major civic and cultural organizations. They make the largest political campaign contributions. They occupy key federal government positions in the executive, legislative, and judicial branches."[45]

This institutional influence explains why, even if most elites do not see themselves as "elites," their voices carry enormous weight in American society. Dye estimates that around 4,000 individuals occupy the highest rungs of these networks—the peak of the Elite One Percent. Many are drawn from Ivy League and "Ivy Plus" schools, with roughly 20 percent attending Harvard and about half attending other prestigious institutions.[46]

Politically, the Elite One Percent lean heavily Democratic: Roughly 70 percent identify with the party, compared with 21 percent who identify as Republican.[47] Yet partisan labels within this group do not always carry the same meaning that they do for everyday voters, such as the two Midwestern women described earlier. Among the general electorate, only 11 percent of Republicans and 20 percent of Democrats believe Americans have too much freedom. Among the Elite One Percent, however, a plurality of Republican elites (43 percent) and a majority of Democratic elites (52 percent) share that view.

A quick calculation shows that Republican elites are roughly thirty-two points more likely than Republican voters to say Americans enjoy too much individual freedom. Democratic elites show a similar gap: They are also thirty-two points more likely than their party's voters to hold the same view. The exact numbers fluctuate, but parallel gaps between party elites and their constituents are common.

---

45 Ibid., p. 10

46 Ibid., p. 180

47 September 11-26, 2023— Napolitan Institute survey of 1,000 elites.

These gaps almost always indicate that elites favor more government authority than the average voter. In other words, voters and elites often inhabit different political worlds. For this reason, caution is warranted when interpreting partisan labels in discussions of the divide between the Elite One Percent and the broader electorate.

For a pollster, reviewing crosstabs and demographic breakdowns is routine—like getting out of bed and having a cup of coffee. While some demographic details were intriguing, a closer look revealed what truly sets the Elite One Percent apart: their strong trust in government.

As noted in the previous chapter, seven out of ten members of the Elite One Percent trust the government to do the right thing most of the time. Among the broader American public, eight out of ten do not.

Trust matters more than most people realize. Research shows that most of what we "see" doesn't come directly through our eyes. To process information efficiently, our brains take in fragments of what's before us and fill in the rest with expectations and assumptions.[48]

Consider a breaking-news video. With a Fox News logo, some viewers accept it as indisputably true; others dismiss it outright. Swap in a CNN logo, and partisan perceptions often flip. The same principle applies to symbols of political identity: a MAGA hat or ICE jacket prompts immediate judgments among political junkies, even before they know what the story says. Conversely, a Black Lives Matter sign or a "Defund the Police" banner triggers opposite reactions.

Ultimately, what we see is shaped by what we expect to see—and what we expect is shaped by whom we trust. When the Elite One Percent surveys the world, they are not seeing the America that most voters see. Dye's work underscores this point: The institutions they inhabit amplify their worldview, creating a feedback loop across

[48] Ed Catmull and Amy Wallace, *Creativity, Inc.* (Random House: 2014).

media, academia, government, and corporate networks that reinforces elite priorities.

Sixty percent of Politically Active Elites believe that working for the government is more "honorable" than working in the private sector.[49] Among the general electorate, almost no one shares that view—aside from those who work in government themselves.[50] Talk about a disconnect.

The more we studied the Elite One Percent, the more convinced I became that we were closing in on the root cause of the toxic political environment threatening our nation. We were beginning to see why elected politicians repeatedly refused to implement policies supported by 70 to 80 percent of voters—and perhaps even who was behind the extreme partisan polarization so often blamed on Donald Trump.

Yet something nagged at me.

I had come to view the battle for America's future as a clash between the American people, who embrace the nation's founding ideals, and a small group of elitists seeking to overturn them. This was the struggle political scientist Aaron Wildavsky foresaw more than fifty years ago in his book *The Revolt Against the Masses*. Certain elites, it seemed, were mounting a counterrevolution against the Declaration of Independence itself.

If that was the case—and I believe it is—how did it produce the longest stretch of close elections in our nation's history? Something didn't add up. Forty years of tight races, split almost evenly between Republicans and Democrats, begged a closer look:

- Republicans won five of the ten elections; Democrats won five.
- Only one Republican and one Democrat exceeded 51 percent of the vote.

[49] March 6-12, 2024, Napolitan Institute survey of 1,500 elites

[50] March 11-12, 2024, Napolitan Institute survey of 1,000 Registered Voters.

- Across those ten presidential contests, 1.2 billion votes were cast. Democrats took 49 percent; Republicans, 47 percent.[51]

With so much common ground among voters, this forty-year stalemate seemed downright peculiar. Why couldn't either party capture even a modest majority for a sustained period? Why wouldn't either side align with voters to secure a decisive victory and unify the country?

This line of inquiry brought me back to the core riddle: how two Midwestern women, sharing so many values, became political opponents.

The lifelong friends agreed on a wide range of issues—issues the Political Class largely ignored or rejected. They both upheld America's founding ideals, the very principles the elitists seemed intent on overturning. Yet they failed to see themselves as political allies, united against the forces threatening those ideals.

Viewed through this lens, the twenty-first-century political landscape starts to resemble a real-life version of *The Hunger Games.* America today is far wealthier than the mythical Panem, but the parallels are striking.

In the 2012 film, the Capitol feasted on the labor and suffering of the outlying Districts. Similarly, five of the seven wealthiest counties in the United States encircle the nation's capital, Washington, D.C.[52]

Like both political parties today, President Snow in *The Hunger Games* relied on false but comforting propaganda, giving his allies talking points to ignore inconvenient truths and sleep better at night. In modern America, Team Red and Team Blue each have their own

---

51 Leip, Election Atlas.

52 "List of highest-income counties in the United States citing 2020 census data," Wikipedia, accessed December 4, 2025, https://en.wikipedia.org/wiki/List_of_highest-income_counties_in_the_United_States citing 2020census data.

media outlets and echo chambers to reassure themselves of their righteousness and the other side's malevolence.

Most importantly, Snow's strategy was to keep the Districts fighting each other—too divided to unite in rebellion. Today, the same tactic, whether deliberate or systemic, keeps Americans so polarized that shared values rarely translate into political solidarity.

That's how rulers have maintained power throughout history. Louis XIV built Versailles to keep nobles jockeying for position rather than plotting against him. Slaveholders in the American South deliberately sowed dissent between poor Whites and enslaved Black people. Stalin mastered the art, ruling the Soviet Union by cultivating fear and enmity within the Communist Party.

In modern America, the Elite One Percent achieve a similar effect—not always consciously, but with the same outcome: Their dominance is rarely challenged. Dye's research shows us why. By controlling media, corporate boards, universities, foundations, policy think tanks, and key government positions, elites reinforce one another's worldview. Their power is structural, not merely personal.

Elites have always had a desperate need to prevent the masses from recognizing their shared strength—a lesson traceable at least as far back as ancient Rome.

During the time of Jesus Christ, the Roman Senate considered requiring slaves to wear distinct clothing for easy identification. Whatever their motives, reality soon intervened: Roughly one-third of the population were slaves, and when freedmen—former slaves—were added, they made up a majority. Senators recognized the danger if the enslaved saw their numerical power, so they rejected the proposal.[53]

[53] Seneca (Lucius Annaeus), *The First Book of the Dialogue of L. Annaeus Seneca,* "Of Clemency," trans. Aubrey Stewart (1900), ca. AD 55, https://en.wikisource.org/wiki/Of_Clemency/Book_I.

America's Political Class today instinctively understands this principle. It's not that they sit around plotting divisions among the public—they rarely think about everyday Americans at all. Instead, the two major parties focus on fighting each other and advancing their agendas. In these Political Class battles, voters are little more than pawns, expendable in the struggle for power.

From the Political Class perspective, America is a 50/50 nation, evenly split between Team Red and Team Blue. Every voter is assumed to be firmly on one side, and anyone who wavers or considers switching teams is treated like a traitor. Elections are viewed as contests of turnout—who can better mobilize their base and get their pawns to the polls?

On the surface, this logic seems sound. It helps explain why the past forty years have produced so many toss-up elections. But the analysis suffers from the same narrow perspective that once made term limits seem "controversial": It looks only at what official Washington cares about—winning and power. From the Capitol's vantage point, voters' actual wants and concerns barely matter.

Things look very different when you start from the perspective of everyday Americans. From that angle, the idea of a 50/50 nation falls apart. A more accurate description might be a 10/10/80 nation: roughly 10 percent on the far left (liberal or progressive) locked in conflict with 10 percent on the far right (conservative or MAGA), while the remaining 80 percent largely keep their heads down, trying to avoid the political crossfire—even if they dutifully cast a ballot on Election Day.

Like most Americans, the two Midwestern women fall within the 80 percent trying to avoid that crossfire. They hold opinions on issues and want to help the nation, but they have no interest in the warfare of politics. Individuals in the 80 percent have different hopes, dreams, and lifestyles, but they share one thing: a desire to live their own lives as they see fit.

Research supports this view. A 2018 report by More in Common identified seven "tribes" in America today. On one extreme are Progressive Activists, about 8 percent of the population. On the other extreme are Devoted Conservatives, roughly 6 percent.[54] Both groups are highly active politically, with a majority treating politics as a hobby. No other tribes in the study are so politically engaged.

Combined, these politically active groups make up just 14 percent of Americans—roughly one in seven voters. Three times as many (41 percent) are neither strongly aligned with the left nor the right. They are politically disengaged or moderate. The remainder are loosely committed conservatives and liberals. Although slightly dated, the findings remain relevant: Roughly two-thirds of Americans are not highly engaged politically and occupy what the report calls the "exhausted majority" of the electorate.

A separate study conducted by the Pew Research Center identified 6 percent of voters as the "progressive left," while 10 percent were classified as "faith and flag conservatives."[55] Similarly, Gallup found that just 10 percent of voters considered themselves "*very conservative*," while 9 percent identified as "very liberal."[56] Taken together, these numbers point to the same conclusion: The active political battles that dominate headlines are fought by only a tiny segment of the American public.

---

[54] Stephen Hawkins et al., "Hidden Tribes: A Study of America's Polarized Landscape," Hidden Tribes, More in Common, 2018, https://hiddentribes.us/?utm_source=substack&utm_medium=email.

[55] "Beyond Red vs. Blue: The Political Typology," Pew Research Center, November 9, 2021, https://www.pewresearch.org/politics/2021/11/09/beyond-red-vs-blue-the-political-typology-2/?utm_source=substack&utm_medium=email.

[56] Megan Brenan, "U.S. Political Parties Historically Polarized Ideologically," Gallup, January 16, 2025, https://news.gallup.com/poll/655190/political-parties-historically-polarized-ideologically.aspx?utm_source=substack&utm_medium=email.

As 2025 came to a close, a Napolitan News survey found that 10 percent of voters preferred Trump- like policies and talked politics most days. On the other side of the aisle, 7 percent preferred AOC-like policies and were that engaged in the political debate. Another 8 percent talk politics most days but prefer more traditional politics (evenly divided between traditional Republicans and traditional Democrats).[57]

For the 80 percent trying to avoid the crossfire, the battle for America's soul is experienced through a political fog of war. Most citizens stand on the periphery of a bitter struggle between two powerful and noisy factions—a confusing conflict that produces constant collateral damage.

Most of the time, we can only see the skirmish directly in front of us—and even then, dimly. Without a sense of the larger picture, we frequently mistake allies, or potential allies, for political opponents.

It is this fog of political war that can make two lifelong Midwestern friends—who share the same hopes, values, and vision for their country—believe they are enemies. It is the fight between the competing political armies that created the riddle of partisan polarization tearing our country apart.

Just how thick that fog has become is evident in the way MAGA voters might label one of these women a RINO and the other something worse. Conversely, neither woman would spend time with—or say anything kind about—the MAGA crowd. Yet most MAGA voters agree with both women—and with the overwhelming majority of voters—on a wide range of issues and core values.

It might sound like a bad joke: A MAGA voter, a RINO, and a Democrat walk into a bar and discover they agree on most things. But the data tells the truth: On fundamental issues, they have far more in common with one another than with the Political Class. The fog of political war is what makes them see each other as enemies.

---

57 December 1-22, 2025—Napolitan News survey of 7,215 registered voters

In *The Hunger Games,* the combatants from the Districts prevailed only when they remembered who the real enemy was. Americans today would do well to do the same.

The problem is, the real enemy doesn't wear a hat, wave a banner, or sit on the other side of the aisle. The real enemy is far less visible—and far more powerful—than anyone wants to admit.

Chapter 4

POLITICALLY ACTIVE ELITES

As my search continued, it became clear that offensive elitist views were far more common among the Elite One Percent than among the public at large. Yet it was important to avoid caricature. Not everyone inside that bubble rejected America's founding ideals. In fact, I found it somewhat encouraging that 21 percent of the Elite One Percent admitted there is *too little* individual freedom in America today.[58]

That small glimmer of hope raised a natural question: Could we persuade *those* few elites to stand up against their more troubling peers? Could they become allies in the fight for freedom, equality, and self-governance?

Before dwelling on that possibility, however, I had to return to the real adversary—a group I long ago labeled the Political Class.

Decades earlier, political scientist Herbert McCloskey defined the Political Class as "those people who occupy themselves with public affairs to an unusual degree."[59] He was referring to government officials, elected officeholders, party activists, publicists, association

---

[58] September 11–26, 2023—Napolitan Institute Survey of 1000 Elites.

[59] Herbert McClosky, "Consensus and Ideology in American Politics," *The American Political Science Review* 58, no. 2 (June 1964): 361–382, https://doi.org/10.2307/1952868.

officers, and opinion leaders.[60] It was a useful definition—and it still fits today.

It also aligns with the framework I've used throughout this book: the idea of a 10/10/80 nation. A narrow band of activists live and breathe politics. They spend their days fighting their ideological opposites. The other 80 percent of Americans simply want to live their lives without being dragged into endless partisan skirmishes.

Our research confirms just how narrow that band truly is. Only about 8 percent of voters talk politics every day. That's certainly an "unusual degree" of interest. By contrast, 69 percent talk politics no more than once a week—including 46 percent who discuss politics less than weekly. Nearly a third of voters—30 percent—broach the subject rarely or never.[61]

Put another way: For every one American who talks politics daily, there are eight who bring it up only once a week or less. And there are four times as many people who rarely or never talk politics as there are daily debaters.

That imbalance matters. It suggests that a tiny group—the people who can't stop talking about politics—sets the tone for the entire national debate. For clarity, I consider these highly engaged partisans a rough approximation of the *Political Class*. The definition is not exact—like fair-weather sports fans, partisans become more vocal when their side is winning. Still, the basic dynamic holds: a small set of activists drives the conversation while the vast majority of Americans keep their distance.

If the Political Class is defined as those with an unusual degree of interest in politics, logic suggests there should be a great deal of overlap with the *Elite One Percent*. Our research confirmed it. Among voters who talk politics daily, fully 50 percent say they trust the federal government to do the right thing most of the time. That's not quite

---

60 Ibid.

61 August 1–31, 2025—Napolitan Institute Survey of 8, 349 registered voters.

as extreme as the 70 percent trust level among the Elite One Percent, but it is worlds apart from the attitudes of most Americans.

Among the vast majority of ordinary citizens—those who talk politics once a week or less—barely one in ten expresses such trust.[62] The contrast could not be starker: Daily talkers and elites put their faith in government; everyone else assumes Washington will let them down.

This realization led me to focus on a very specific subset: members of the Elite One Percent who also talk politics daily. These are the *Politically Active Elites,* and they are even further out of touch with the public than other elites. An astonishing 89 percent of them trust the federal government most of the time. Even more jaw-dropping, 69 percent believe the rest of us enjoy too much individual freedom.[63]

Who are these people? If men are from Mars and women are from Venus, Politically Active Elites must be orbiting in another solar system altogether.

At this point, my suspicion hardened. Perhaps the true enemy was not the Elite One Percent as a whole but this narrower band of Politically Active Elites. Their worldview—rooted in government trust and hostility to individual liberty—stood in direct opposition to the nation's founding ideals.

That suspicion grew stronger when I examined education.

Across America, a powerful parental-choice movement is sweeping the country. Since 2019, the number of students benefiting from school-choice programs has more than doubled.[64] The reason is clear:

---

62 Ibid.

63 September 11-26, 2023— Napolitan Institute survey of 1,000 elites.

64 Dana Goldstein and Sarah Mervosh, "School Vouchers Won in Texas. Next Up, the Nation," *The New York Times,* April 17, 2025, https://www.nytimes.com/2025/04/17/us/school-choice-trump.html.

Most voters (62 percent) believe parents have too little control over their children's education.[65]

But once again, politically active elites stand apart. By a margin of three to one, they insist that parents already wield too much control.[66] At a moment when parents are demanding more involvement in their children's schooling, elitists are pushing in the opposite direction.

This gap was dramatically illustrated in the 2021 race for governor of Virginia. Former Democratic governor Terry McAuliffe entered the campaign as the clear favorite against Republican businessman Glenn Youngkin. Virginia was considered reliably blue; just a year earlier, Joe Biden had carried the state by ten points.

Then came a moment that changed everything. During their second televised debate, McAuliffe declared, "I don't think parents should be telling schools what they should teach."[67] It was a stunning line. The Youngkin campaign instantly recognized that McAuliffe had handed them political gold. Within hours, they cut ads replaying the remark, and by mid-October it had become the centerpiece of the Republican message.

McAuliffe's team, by contrast, seemed oblivious. They failed to grasp the damage the comment had done—and in truth, they never really did. Just days before the election, McAuliffe doubled down, insisting, "People trust me on education."[68] Voters didn't. Exit polls

---

[65] March 25–26, 2024—Napolitan Institute data from survey of 1,000 registered voters.

[66] April 23–28, 2024—Napolitan Institute data from survey of 500 elites.

[67] "User Clip: Terry McAuliffe: 'I Don't Think Parents Should Be Telling Schools What They Should Teach,'" C-SPAN, September 28, 2021, https://www.c-span.org/clip/public-affairs-event/user-clip-terry-mcauliffe-i-dont-think-parents-should-be-telling-schools-what-they-should-teach/4979586.

[68] Chuck Todd, "Meet the Press – October 31, 2021," NBC News, https://www.nbcnews.com/meet-the-press/news/meet-press-october-31-2021-n1282808.

showed that only one in ten Virginians agreed with his stance on parental involvement.[69] Talk about misreading the room.

How could a seasoned political operative misjudge the public mood so badly? The answer lay in the bubble of the Politically Active Elites. McAuliffe had chaired presidential campaigns for Bill and Hillary Clinton, run the Democratic National Committee, and served a term as governor. His entire career had been spent inside the world of political insiders.

Within that world, his debate remark was not controversial. Quite the opposite: Among Politically Active Elites—especially Democratic operatives and progressive activists—the idea that education should be left to "professionals" was considered self-evident. One supporter put it bluntly: "When it comes to what is being taught, that should be left up to elected and appointed professionals."[70] Another echoed the sentiment: "Parents should stay out of the classroom and let us decide what to teach our students."[71]

To ordinary Virginians, those words dripped with arrogance. To the insiders, they sounded like common sense. That gulf—between how elites heard McAuliffe's comment and how voters heard it—proved fatal to his campaign.

Even if McAuliffe's allies believed he was right, it is striking that his campaign failed to respond more effectively as polls showed the issue gaining traction. While Youngkin steadily climbed, McAuliffe's team dismissed the danger. They were blinded by the very problem

---

69. "Virginia Governor Election Results 2021: Youngkin Wins," NBC News, November 2, 2021, https://www.nbcnews.com/politics/2021-elections/virginia-governor-results/.

70. Matt Walton, "I'm a teacher. Parents should stay out of the classroom and let us decide what to teach our students," *Business Insider*, October 13, 2021, https://www.businessinsider.com/parents-critical-race-theory-teacher-schools-curriculums-terry-mcauliffe-virginia-2021-10.

71. Ibid.

I described in the previous chapter: Only part of what we see comes through our eyes; the rest we fill in with what we expect to see.

Inside McAuliffe's orbit, Politically Active Elites simply could not grasp how out of touch their candidate sounded. At the same time, they viewed conservative Republicans as deplorable, even racist. Instead of recognizing voter frustration, they saw what they expected to see and accused Youngkin of peddling racist "dog whistles." Liberal media outlets like PBS and *The Washington Post* echoed the line, insisting the controversy was really about opposition to critical race theory—while at the same time claiming that critical race theory wasn't being taught in Virginia schools.

The result was predictable: The campaign never corrected course. Their blindness cost them an election they should have won easily.

The episode underscores a larger truth: Politically Active Elites rarely recognize just how wildly disconnected their views are from those of the American people. Because they overwhelmingly trust the government, 75 percent of them mistakenly believe that most voters share that view.[72] It's hard to overstate how wrong they are.

This "trust gap" is a foundational problem in American politics, though elitists themselves are scarcely aware it exists. Consider one telling data point: 60 percent of politically active elites say working for government is more "honorable" than working in the private sector.[73] For people with that worldview, protecting teachers and bureaucrats from parental scrutiny seems noble. In reality, it was political suicide.

Their misjudgment goes even deeper. A staggering 82 percent of Politically Active Elites believe that most people agree with them on most important issues.[74] It is hard to imagine a more delusional assumption. But that illusion explains a great deal about the dysfunc-

---

[72] April 23–28, 20—Napolitan Institute survey of 1,000 elites.

[73] March 6–12, 2024—Napolitan Institute survey of 1,000 elites.

[74] Ibid.

tion of our political system. McAuliffe's team could not comprehend why voters reacted so strongly to his education remark—because in their world, it sounded perfectly reasonable.

The trust gap between Politically Active Elites and everyday Americans is rooted in the very different relationships voters and elites have with government.

For most voters, the relationship is one-sided. They are expected to follow government rules but are largely ignored when it comes to writing those rules. Only 11 percent of voters believe their own representative in Congress would be very likely to consider their views on an issue they cared about.[75] From what I've seen, even that 11 percent may be overly optimistic. When only one in nine Americans think their elected official is listening, the title "Representative" begins to sound more like wishful branding than reality.

Elites live in a different world. Most already know their member of Congress—or know someone who can arrange an introduction. As a result, 65 percent of Politically Active Elites believe it is very likely their views will be taken seriously.[76] Additionally, political leaders and well-connected insiders routinely ignore the very rules they wrote for everyone else to follow.

This divide produces two alternate realities. Ordinary voters—the 80 percent who keep their heads down—are content to stay out of partisan crossfire. Elitists, meanwhile, are equally content to remain in their bubble, ignoring voters while plotting ways to "own" the opposing political team.

Most of the time, this trust gap simmers quietly. If elitists pursue abstract or symbolic agendas, everyday Americans shrug them off. But when those agendas intrude on daily life—when they impact and offend ordinary people—the result can be explosive.

---

75 March 11–12, 2024—Napolitan Institute survey of 1,000 registered voters.

76 March 6–12, 2024—Napolitan Institute survey of 1,000 Members of the Elite One Percent.

The trust gap is like a brushfire waiting for a match. It only takes one spark to set it off, and that's exactly what happened to Terry McAuliffe's campaign in Virginia. This was not a theoretical debate about the relationship between parents, teachers, and school boards. It was not a policy discussion about how to improve math instruction or raise test scores. It became something much bigger: a cultural battle, ignited when elitists sought to impose their ideology on an unsuspecting community.

The match that ignited Virginia's brushfire in 2021 was a decision by the Loudoun County school board to allow high school students to use the bathroom matching their self-identified gender. Most voters only became aware of the policy after a skirt-wearing male student used the girls' bathroom and sexually assaulted a 15-year-old girl.[77] At first, school officials tried to cover up what had happened. When the truth emerged, parents were rightly outraged.

A rational response from the school system would have been to reconsider the policy and reassure parents that student safety came first. Perhaps there should have been an investigation into how such an unpopular and risky policy was adopted in the first place. Polling shows that voters overwhelmingly reject the idea of biological boys using girls' bathrooms, with strong majorities recognizing that it puts women and girls in danger.[78]

But Loudoun officials did none of this. Instead, they defended the policy, downplayed the assault, and attacked parents who dared to complain. In one infamous incident, they even had the victim's father arrested after he demanded accountability for what had happened to his daughter.[79]

---

[77] Joe Concha, "Education blunder igniting suburban parents driving McAuliffe panic in Virginia," *The Hill*, October 28, 2021, https://thehill.com/opinion/campaign/578885-education-blunder-igniting-suburban-parents-driving-mcauliffe-panic-in/.

[78] March 23–24, 2023—Napolitan Institute survey of 1,000 registered voters.

[79] Concha, "Education blunder."

This was the context in which Virginia parents demanded more control over their children's education. They weren't debating abstractions about school governance. They wanted their children to be safe—from both physical harm and ideological imposition. That reality was invisible to McAuliffe's team, blinded by the worldview of Politically Active Elites.

One reason for the blind spot is cultural drift. Among Politically Active Elites, 61 percent say they have introduced themselves by stating their preferred pronouns—a hallmark of progressive identity politics. For them, it's routine. For ordinary Americans, it is not. Nationwide, only 10 percent of voters have ever introduced themselves that way.[80]

The same pattern shows up on the question of biological males competing in women's sports. Within the elite bubble, the issue is "controversial": 41 percent of Politically Active Elites say males should be allowed to compete, while 51 percent disagree.[81] Among voters at large, it isn't controversial at all. Just 13 percent support letting biological males into women's sports; 87 percent reject the idea outright.[82]

Given all this, it is worth asking why the Loudoun County School Board—and so many other governing bodies—implement and defend policies that are deeply unpopular with the public. The answer is that within their elite bubble, such policies are not unpopular at all. Surrounded by like-minded peers, they mistake fringe ideas for mainstream values. Then, when mainstream voters notice and push back, the elites are shocked and dismayed.

This disconnect is not new. More than half a century ago, political scientist Aaron Wildavsky observed that a "white, radical,

---

80 March 6–7, 2024-- Napolitan Institute survey of 1,000 registered voters and March 6–12, 2024—Napolitan Institute survey of 1,500 elites.

81 March 6–7, 2024—Napolitan Institute data from survey of 1,000 elites.

82 May 14–15, 2024—Napolitan Institute data from survey of 1,000 registered voters.

privileged elite" sought to purge society "of the values, tastes, preferences, and policies desired by the mass of Americans."[83] Elites were offended that ordinary Americans dare to challenge their authority and viewed mainstream choices—even something as basic as keeping boys in the boys' room—as backward or intolerant.

Wildavsky saw the problem clearly as the turbulence of the 1960s faded. Members of the radical elite, he noted, were "characterized by enormous hostility to what they perceive as the idiocy of mass taste. They despise everything about the masses."[84] His warning was blunt: "The white elite is in revolt against the masses."[85]

A generation later, historian Christopher Lasch offered a similar but updated critique. The "new elites," he wrote, were "in revolt against Middle America" itself. To them, America was "technologically backward, politically reactionary, repressive in its sexual morality, middlebrow in its tastes, smug and complacent, dull and dowdy." Rather than identify with the heartland, they cultivated "ties with the international market in fast-moving money, glamour, fashion, and popular culture." Lasch even wondered aloud whether they thought of themselves as Americans at all.[86]

Our research on the Elite One Percent confirms what Wildavsky and Lasch warned decades ago. The disdain elites feel toward ordinary Americans is so deep that half of the Elite One Percent (51 percent) believe the nation would be better off if only college graduates were allowed to vote.[87] Apparently, they think people without degrees simply aren't voting the "right" way.

---

83 Aaron Wildavsky, *The Revolt Against the Masses* (Routledge: 2002), 29.

84 *Revolt*, 30.

85 *Revolt*, 29.

86 Christopher Lasch, *The Revolt of the Elites and the Betrayal of Democracy* (W. W. Norton & Co.: 1996, Revised Ed.).

87 March 6–12, 2024—Napolitan Institute survey of 1,000 members of the Elite One Percent.

Among Politically Active Elites—those who obsess over politics daily and drive the national conversation—the contempt runs even deeper. Sixty-nine percent of them say only college graduates should be allowed to cast a ballot.[88]

This is one of those survey results that requires a moment to sink in. Just 37 percent of American adults hold a college degree; 63 percent do not.[89] Which means two-thirds of Politically Active Elites would disenfranchise a clear majority of their fellow citizens. Talk about un-American. In fact, the attitude is disturbingly reminiscent of the "literacy tests" used in the Jim Crow South to strip Black Americans of their right to vote.

My search for the real enemy had brought me closer to the truth. The overlap between the Elite One Percent, the Political Class, and the Politically Active Elites was both fascinating and alarming. And the trust gap was even more significant than I had imagined—not only because everyday Americans mistrust Washington, but because elitists themselves trust government almost blindly.

I was on to something, but the picture was not yet complete. To understand how this new class of elitists threatens self-governance, I needed to explore the world of Politically Active Elites even further—and see exactly how the forces Wildavsky and Lasch described have taken shape in twenty-first-century America.

---

88 Ibid

89 "Census Bureau Releases New Educational Attainment Data," Census Bureau, press release, February 16, 2023, https://www.census.gov/newsroom/press-releases/2023/educational-attainment-data.html.

Chapter 5

GROUPTHINK, ARROGANCE, AND CENSORSHIP

The cultural gatekeepers who dream of purging society of mainstream values, tastes, and traditions recently met their match in…a jeans ad.

On July 23, 2025, American Eagle launched a national campaign featuring actress Sydney Sweeney. In the flagship video—echoed in print ads and on billboards—she zipped up a pair of jeans while delivering a playful monologue: "Genes are passed down from parents to offspring.… My jeans are blue." The tagline read, *"Sydney Sweeney has great jeans."*

Within hours, the rollout became a culture-war flashpoint. *Adweek* reported that the brand was "facing a media firestorm" and had made a "jarring misstep."[90] Progressive critics claimed the pun—paired with Sweeney's blonde hair and blue eyes—echoed Nazi propaganda or White-supremacist imagery.

---

[90] Rebecca Steward and Robert Klara, "How American Eagle's Sydney Sweeney Ads Became a Culture War Flashpoint," *Adweek,* July 29, 2025, https://www.adweek.com/brand-marketing/how-american-eagles-sydney-sweeney-ads-became-a-culture-war-flashpoint/.

Inside the political bubble, the outrage was intense. Nearly half (44 percent) of Americans with "an unusual interest" in politics followed the story very closely. Among those who discuss politics daily, opinion split evenly: 48 percent said the ad promoted racist propaganda; 43 percent disagreed.[91]

Outside that bubble, however, America shrugged. Among voters who rarely talk politics, only 8 percent were paying close attention. By a six-to-one margin, these politically disengaged Americans dismissed the controversy, seeing nothing more than an actress in a denim ad.[92] Only 12 percent of all voters nationwide said it was propaganda for racist views. Across party lines, majorities of both Republicans and Democrats agreed it was just advertising.[93]

The contrast is telling. Political insiders saw a crisis; ordinary citizens saw a commercial. The episode illustrates what Christopher Lasch called "the growing insularity of elites"—a class increasingly detached from the daily concerns, and the common sense, of the people they claim to lead.[94] And this was only a jeans ad. The stakes grow far higher when elite groupthink turns from clothing campaigns to questions of speech, education, and governance.

Among political elites, the American Eagle campaign became an ideological battleground. Everyday Americans—if they noticed it at all—shrugged. To them, it was just another ad for blue jeans.

Most people also recognize a simple truth: Sex sells, and advertising exists to sell. Yet even this basic reality unsettled some elite commentators. *The Wall Street Journal* quoted brand experts who scolded the campaign for leaning on "a dated sexuality that was

---

[91] August 6–7, 2025—Napolitan News survey of 1,000 registered voters

[92] August 6–7, 2025—Napolitan News survey of 1,000 registered voters

[93] Ibid.

[94] Lasch, *Revolt*, 80.

common in ads of the past." Their conclusion: "People just don't buy it anymore."[95]

But in reality, the brand knew exactly what it was doing. By playing on a cultural touchstone and pushing just enough to provoke, American Eagle could count on elites to be triggered—and on media to amplify the controversy. Once the chatter reached ordinary Americans, most shrugged at the supposed scandal. But thanks to the saturation coverage, they also knew exactly where to buy the jeans.

The results spoke for themselves. In the first week, Sweeney's custom jeans sold out. Her jacket disappeared in a single day.[96] Within six weeks, her "Syd's Picks" shop online had been restocked four times. American Eagle's chief marketing officer called it the company's "most successful campaign to date," reporting "unprecedented new customer acquisition" and sales gains "in every single county in the U.S."[97]

Investors were just as surprised as the critics were dismissive. On the day results were announced, American Eagle's stock surged 38 percent.[98]

Even after that reality check, the elitist cultural warriors still didn't get it. In a video interview conducted five months later, GQ reporter Katherine Stoeffel repeatedly tried to get Sweeney to apologize

---

[95] Megan Graham, "American Eagle's Male-Geared Sydney Sweeney Ads Have Gen Z Women Scratching Their Heads," *The Wall Street Journal*, July 31, 2024, https://www.wsj.com/articles/american-eagles-male-geared-sydney-sweeney-ads-have-gen-z-women-scratching-their-heads-3c116d82.

[96] Hilary George, "American Eagle's Sydney Sweeney campaign is its 'most successful to date' despite backlash," *Page Six*, September 4, 2025, https://pagesix.com/2025/09/04/style/american-eagles-sydney-sweeney-campaign-is-its-most-successful-yet/.

[97] Ibid.

[98] Todd Campbell, "American Eagle stock surges 38% on earnings surprise," *The Street*, September 4, 2025, https://www.thestreet.com/retail/american-eagle-stock-surges-30-on-celebrity-collabs.

for that ad. When the actress made clear that she had nothing to apologize for, BuzzFeed claimed that "people are even more outraged."[99]

Outside of the elitist bubble, though, people weren't outraged. Instead, they were buying jeans and the success of the ad campaign was clearly visible. By year end, American Eagles's stock price had nearly tripled.

In many ways, the elite misunderstanding of the Sydney Sweeney campaign echoed the Bud Light debacle of 2023. Bud Light had been the world's bestselling beer, built on an image of lighthearted, even "fratty," humor. But the brand's vice president of marketing at the time, Alissa Heinerscheid, dismissed that heritage as a "hangover" and insisted it was "really important that we had another approach."[100] Her effort to "evolve and elevate" the brand by making it more "inclusive" backfired badly: Bud Light sales plunged by 30 percent, and the longtime market leader fell to number three.[101]

In both cases, elites and experts misread the country. They looked at products ordinary Americans embraced and decided those choices needed to be corrected or improved. And ordinary Americans recoiled at the arrogance.

The reaction may seem out of proportion to the ad campaigns themselves. But as marriage counselors often note, when a small

---

[99] Stephanie Soteriou, "People Are Even More Outraged Over Sydney Sweeney's Dismissive Comments About The American Eagle "Eugenics" Backlash After Seeing New Footage Of Her Response," *Buzzfeed,* November 7, 2025, https://www.yahoo.com/entertainment/celebrity/articles/people-even-more-outraged-over-122131218.html

[100] Alexander Hall, "Bud Light's marketing VP says she was inspired to update 'fratty,' 'out of touch' branding with inclusivity," Fox News, April 10, 2023, https://www.foxnews.com/media/bud-light-marketing-vp-inspired-update-fratty-touch-branding-inclusivity.

[101] Agustin Hays, "Bud Light hasn't recovered from Mulvaney controversy, ex-Anheuser-Busch exec says," FOXBusiness, February 7, 2025, https://www.foxbusiness.com/media/bud-light-hasnt-recovered-from-mulvaney-controversy-ex-anheuser-busch-exec-says.

incident sparks an outsized emotional response, it usually touches a deeper issue. Here, the deeper issue was cultural: elites were unhappy with the country as it is, and ordinary citizens were resentful of elites trying to remake American culture.

In the grand scheme of things, it doesn't matter much if marketing experts help or hurt their companies. If Bud Light stumbles, another brand steps in. And in politics, voters have a remedy: Terry McAuliffe lost because he misread parents.

But it matters a great deal when Politically Active Elites misread the country and still hold institutional power—in schools, bureaucracies, media, and foundations—with little accountability. That's when their preferences harden into rules for everyone else.

How out of touch are they?

Start with the issue that helped sink McAuliffe: gender identity in schools. If a child tells a teacher he or she is considering a new gender identity, 74 percent of Politically Active Elites say teachers should be prohibited from notifying the child's parents.[102] Voters take the opposite view: a strong majority (73 percent) say schools should be required to notify parents.[103] The gap isn't subtle; it's foundational—who raises children: parents or the system?

Zoom out to education priorities. Voters overwhelmingly say it's more important to create good jobs for people without a college degree than to push everyone toward college. They also want every high school graduate to read, write, and function as an adult—and if a student hasn't acquired those basic skills, they shouldn't graduate.

Among Politically Active Elites, consensus breaks down. Forty-four percent say getting everyone to college is more important than

---

[102] June 13-14, 2024— Napolitan Institute data from survey of 1,000 elites.

[103] November 13, 2024— Napolitan News data from survey of 1,000 registered voters.

creating good jobs. And 49 percent would still award a diploma to someone who hasn't mastered basic skills.[104]

That's the divide: Voters ask for parental authority, competence, and practical opportunity; elites push credentialism and ideology. When the latter controls policy, backlash is not a surprise—it's inevitable.

These attitudes line up with an even starker tell: A majority of Politically Active Elites say only college graduates should be allowed to vote—a twenty-first-century echo of literacy tests. It signals thin respect for the Americans who choose other paths. The same mindset helps explain how anyone could defend handing out a high school diploma to students who haven't mastered basic skills.

The gap between Politically Active Elites and the rest of the nation is troubling. What makes it dangerous is that elites don't see the gap at all. As noted earlier, 82 percent believe most Americans agree with them on important issues.

How can they be so wrong? As Princeton scholars Frances E. Lee and Stephen Macedo observe, elite networks are prone to groupthink and the mutual reinforcement of bias.[105] In American history, that dynamic helped pave the way for misjudgments from the Bay of Pigs to Vietnam to the Iraq War. Groupthink, they write, is "fed by a self-righteous sense of moral and intellectual superiority."[106] That description fits today's progressive, Democratic-leaning insiders all too well.

It also shows up in how they want the country governed: 56 percent of Politically Active Elites trust government experts over voters and their elected representatives when setting rules and regulations.[107]

---

[104] Napolitan Institute, "Elite 1 Percent."

[105] Frances Lee and Stephen Macedo, *In Covid's Wake: How Our Politics Failed Us* (Blackstone Publishing, Inc.: 2025), 25.

[106] Ibid.

[107] Napolitan Institute, "Elite 1 Percent," p. 12

Main Street Americans see it differently. By 55 to 24 percent, they place their trust in voters and elected representatives. "Main Street Americans" are the overwhelming majority who don't have any of the elite attributes. They don't have a postgraduate degree, don't live in densely populated urban cores, and earn less than $150,000 a year. They still believe in the country's founding ideals and expect government to work for them. Progressive elites, by contrast, prefer rule by credential—the Harvard-style answer to every argument: *Why won't they just let us lead?*

And when people who think that way gain control of schools, agencies, and information platforms, disagreement isn't something to debate—it's something to manage and suppress.

The problem isn't only what progressive elitists believe; it's where they want to take the country—and how certain they are that everyone else wants to go along.

To "fight climate change," Politically Active Elites overwhelmingly favor bans on gas-powered cars (88 percent), gas stoves (87 percent), SUVs (84 percent), nonessential air travel (84 percent), and even private air conditioning (82 percent). Voters reject each of these by wide margins: 70 to 83 percent oppose banning any of them.[108]

Even more telling, elites imagine the public is with them. Fifty-three percent of Politically Active Elites believe most voters favor regulations that would effectively outlaw gasoline-powered cars.[109]

The same pattern appears on guns. Nearly eight in ten Politically Active Elites favor banning private gun ownership (76 percent), and a similar share say they'd prefer to live in communities where guns are outlawed (70 percent).[110] One again, most of these elitists (57 percent) think most Americans share their views.[111] Once again, they

---

[108] Ibid, p.16
[109] Ibid, p.16
[110] Ibid, p 15
[111] Ibid, p 21

are wrong. Most Americans prefer to live in communities where guns are allowed.[112]

Simply put, elite intuitions about public opinion are no better than their read on the Sydney Sweeney campaign: confident, insular—and wrong.

The elitist misunderstanding of the nation they want to rule is reminiscent of King George III's mistaken belief that the southern colonies would help him defeat the troublemakers in Boston.

Ultimately, it comes back to the trust gap. Public distrust isn't a vague mood; it shapes every part of our politics. During COVID, a trustworthy government would have helped. Instead, 67 percent of voters believe the government intentionally released false and misleading information.[113] When people stop trusting, they stop complying—and those in power reach for control. That's where groupthink hardens into censorship.

That judgment goes well beyond "mistakes were made." Two-thirds of voters are saying the government intentionally fed the public false information.

As professors Lee and Macedo note, many public-health experts and elite scientists likely believed they were acting in the public interest.[114] It was a twenty-first-century version of Plato's "noble lie." Policymakers who lie for what they deem the common good typically assume ordinary citizens "are unable to evaluate properly" the serious matters being decided.[115]

The noble lies backfired. They deepened distrust. Despite strenuous attempts to smother discussion of a lab-leak origin in Wuhan, most Americans continued to see it as the likeliest explanation.[116]

---

[112] Sept 3, 2025, Napolitan News data from survey of 1,000 registered voters.
[113] Sept 6–7, 2023-- Napolitan News data from survey of 1,000 registered voters,
[114] Lee et al., *In Covid's Wake*, 256.
[115] Lee et al., *In Covid's Wake*, 253.
[116] May 27–28, 2022—Napolitan News survey of 1,000 registered voters

Both voters and elites say they worry about "misinformation," but they mean opposite things. Most voters see the federal government as a central source of misinformation because it regularly and intentionally releases it. From that perspective, letting the government decide what counts as misinformation is more dangerous than the misinformation itself.[117] Asking Washington to police speech is like asking Al Capone to guard a bank.

Accordingly, only 16 percent of voters say the federal government should be allowed to censor social-media posts.[118]

In the insular world of Politically Active Elites, the biggest problem is speech the government can't control. They are troubled by people who questioned extended school closures or challenged other policies during the pandemic. So trusting of government are they that 53 percent want Washington to maintain order by defining what can and cannot be said on social media.[119]

This is the trust gap in action.

Frustrated by public resistance, many elites seem to admire the power their counterparts wield elsewhere. Fifty-five percent consider China a force for good in the world, and 54 percent even call it a US ally.[120] That is not just out of touch with voters; it reveals a comfort with top-down control.

A recent *60 Minutes* segment praised Germany's speech laws, under which you can be arrested for insulting someone online or in person. Correspondent Sharyn Alfonsi framed it as "trying to

---

[117] July 30–31, 2025—Napolitan News survey of 1,000 registered voters

[118] March 26–27, 2024—Napolitan Institute survey of 1,000 registered voters.

[119] March 26–27, 2024—Napolitan Institute survey of 1,000 registered voters; March 6–12, 2024—Napolitan Institute survey of 1,500 elites.

[120] Napolitan Institute, "Elite 1 Percent," p. 20

bring some civility" to the web by policing speech "in a way most Americans could never imagine."[121]

There are two reasons most Americans can't imagine it. First, we have the First Amendment's guarantee of free speech—seen as a problem by too many elites. Second, only 22 percent of voters believe such restrictions are appropriate; 69 percent correctly recognize them as censorship.[122] In the same interview, a German official noted you can be punished for calling someone a "son of a b++tch." While Alfonsi lamented that America permits such "toxic" language, 82 percent of US voters say it is protected speech.[123]

To be clear, voters don't endorse hateful language. Most would welcome more civility online and off. But they also understand that handing any government, or any credentialed committee, the power to decide what others may say is a bigger danger than rough words.

Politically Active Elites disagree. Their instinct is to referee the conversation, to install an elite review board—formal or informal—that filters what the public is allowed to see. That impulse takes us from arrogance to something more serious: the urge to police speech.

Making matters worse is the delusional belief among Politically Active Elites that the American people agree with them on most issues. That belief becomes a permission slip to bend rules in service of their agenda. If they tell themselves most voters are on their side, then "bending" looks like acting on the public's behalf.

The most terrifying evidence of that mindset came from a Napolitan Institute question: if your preferred candidate lost a close election and your campaign believed it could get away with cheating to win, would you want them to cheat? Seven percent of voters

---

[121] Alexander Hall, "German prosecutors tell '60 Minutes' it's a crime to insult people online as government raids offenders' homes," Fox News, February 18, 2025, https://www.foxnews.com/media/german-prosecutors-tell-60-minutes-its-crime-insult-people-online-government-raids-offenders-homes.

[122] February 19-20—Napolitan News survey of 1,000 registered voters

[123] Ibid.

said yes.[124] That's not something the two Midwestern women could even imagine; I wish it were closer to 1 or 2 percent, but 7 percent isn't the end of the world. There remains broad support for letting voters decide.

Among the Elite One Percent, support for cheating jumped to 35 percent. Even worse, among the Politically Active Elites, 69 percent would want their team to cheat to win rather than accept the voters' decision.[125] That is the worldview of people who believe they were meant to rule, who reject America's founding ideals, and who treat power as the highest good.

When we first reported these results, Newt Gingrich said that our work had "done America an enormous service." The former House Speaker said we had "identified the driving forces behind the destructive radicalism which is pushing us into a cultural civil war."[126]

I knew we were closing in on the real enemy. But where did this threat to America's founding ideals come from? Who trained a governing class to see the public as an obstacle, elections as optional, and dissent as something to manage? That is the story we turn to next.

---

[124] August 24-25, 2023—Napolitan Institute data from survey of 1,000 registered voters

[125] September 11-26, 2024—Napolitan Institute data from survey of 1,000 elites.

[126] "Newt Gingrich, "GINGRICH: The elite 1 percent behind the cultural civil war," *North State Journal,* February 2, 2024, https://nsjonline.com/article/2024/02/gingrich-the-elite-1-percent-behind-the-cultural-civil-war/.

Chapter 6

DISDAIN FOR THE MASSES

The two Midwestern women grew up with the old American creed: freedom of speech and religion, equal dignity, and self-governance. Those rights felt as natural as breathing—guaranteed by a Constitution that promised a government of, by, and for the people.

They also knew America's sins—slavery, the treatment of Native Americans, and more. The country wasn't perfect, but in their experience, it was great and getting better.

Only lately did they sense something had gone wrong. It snuck up on them—disappointment shading into a little betrayal. What changed? Where was it leading?

They struggled to name it because most Americans are never taught a crucial part of our history: a recurring elitist impulse—visible from the Constitutional Convention onward—that distrusts ordinary citizens.

On June 18, 1787, Alexander Hamilton rose at the Constitutional Convention and spoke for six hours—a moment later immortalized in the Broadway musical *Hamilton.* He had already become one of the most influential founders despite humble beginnings: born in the

Caribbean, orphaned young, a gifted writer and wartime leader who embodied what we now call the American Dream.[127]

At thirty, the Revolutionary War hero had earned his place in the room where the new government was being designed. His life story was admirable; his plan was another matter.

Hamilton proposed that the "Supreme Executive Authority" (what we would call the president) be elected once and serve for life. In a nation that had just thrown off a king, he was effectively arguing for an elected one. An open admirer of the British model, he saw little use for reelection campaigns or term limits.[128]

This came just eleven years after the *Declaration of Independence* asserted that governments derive "their just powers from the consent of the governed." Apparently, to Hamilton (and more than a few of his colleagues), that sounded more like a wartime slogan than a governing constraint.

It wasn't just the president Hamilton wanted serving for life. He thought senators should serve for life as well. In the twenty-first century, we already know what it's like to have too many leaders in their eighties; imagine how much worse it would be if there were no elections and senators simply remained in power until they died.[129]

If that weren't enough, Hamilton didn't think state governors should be elected at all. Rather than being chosen by voters, he believed governors should be appointed by the president and treated

[127] History.com editors, "Alexander Hamilton," accessed December 10, 2025, https://www.history.com/articles/alexander-hamilton.

[128] US Constitutional Convention, "Plan of Government," archived at Founders Online, June 18, 1787, https://founders.archives.gov/documents/Hamilton/01-04-02-0099.

[129] Ibid.

as federal officers.[130] Later, in *The Federalist Papers*, he argued that the government's powers "ought to exist without limitation."[131]

Again, consider the timing. This was less than four years after the Treaty of Paris formally ended the War for Independence, recognizing that the thirteen newly independent states were no longer ruled by a king in London. Hamilton seemed willing to have them ruled by a king in Virginia.

Thankfully, none of the other delegates backed his plan, and it was never revisited. Instead, they embraced James Madison's design, with significant checks and balances on government power. The first Congress quickly strengthened the original Constitution with the Bill of Rights, which has played a pivotal role in our history.

In fairness, Hamilton wasn't alone in distrusting ordinary citizens. Roger Sherman—a central figure of the era—didn't think voters should directly choose their representatives in Congress. He believed the people "should have as little to do as may be about the government."[132]

Looking back, such attitudes seem ridiculous only because we forget how radical the American experiment was—and is. As the Hoover Institution's Bruce Thornton notes, elite "disdain for the masses has been a constant theme of political philosophy for over 2,500 years."[133] Aristotle and Socrates were among those who considered it preposterous that ordinary people could play any role in governing.

---

[130] Ibid.

[131] James Madison and Alexander Hamilton, "Federalist 23," 1788, https://constitutioncenter.org/the-constitution/historic-document-library/detail/james-madison-federalist-no-51-1788.

[132] Bruce Thornton, "Are We Smart Enough for Democracy?" Hoover Institution, February 4, 2015, https://www.hoover.org/research/are-we-smart-enough-democracy.

[133] Ibid.

Today it feels obvious that a free people should choose their rulers. In 1787, it did not. The Philadelphia "miracle" created the world the two Midwestern women took for granted: a structure strong enough to face foreign threats yet broad enough to secure individual rights.

But the disdain never vanished. When Hamilton's bid for lifetime rule failed, a different elite mounted a new assault on the ideals of the Declaration.

South Carolina's John Calhoun, leader of the pro-slavery movement, called the Declaration's claim that all men are created equal a great "error" producing "poisonous fruits."[134] In his view, Black people were "too ignorant, degraded, and vicious" to be worthy of freedom.[135]

It wasn't only equality he rejected. The Yale-educated elitist also denied self-government itself, declaring that "The will of a majority is the will of a rabble." He believed that "democracy is incompatible with liberty."[136] Calhoun's views were widely shared among Southern elites. Their rejection of America's founding ideals ultimately led to eleven states seceding from the Union and provoking the Civil War.

Neither Hamilton nor Calhoun was a fringe figure. Hamilton advised George Washington, served as a general in the War for Independence, and became the nation's first treasury secretary. Calhoun

---

[134] John C. Calhoun, "Speech on the Oregon Bill," Teaching American History, edited and introduced by David Tucker, originally June 27, 1848, https://teachingamericanhistory.org/document/speech-on-the-oregon-bill-3/.

[135] John C. Calhoun, "Disquisition on Government," Teaching American History, 1840, https://teachingamericanhistory.org/document/disquisition-on-government/.

[136] John S. Jenkins, "Calhoun's Views of Slavery, His Character, and His Personality," History Central, accessed December 10, 2025, https://www.historycentral.com/documents/Calhoun.html.

was a US senator and twice vice president; during the Civil War, Confederate currency even bore his likeness.[137]

Abraham Lincoln captured the danger posed by elitist opposition to America's founding ideals. Speaking at Gettysburg, he described the Civil War as a test of whether a nation "conceived in Liberty, and dedicated to the proposition that all men are created equal…can long endure."[138]

We've come a long way since Lincoln, but we are being tested again. The future our children and grandchildren inherit is not yet settled. I remain an optimist and believe our nation's best days are ahead, but the strength of today's elitist revolt shouldn't be underestimated.

The good news is that our founding ideals remain deeply embedded in the American mind. Eighty-five percent of voters agree that "all people are endowed by their Creator with certain unalienable rights, that among these are life, liberty, and the pursuit of happiness."[139]

That shared creed is America's cultural DNA—the source of our unity and our resilience. Because the people have embraced these ideals, the United States has prospered for two and a half centuries and become known worldwide as a land of opportunity. Looking ahead, that conviction is the best reason to believe we can defeat the elitist revolt.

But we can't win until we clearly recognize the threat. The un-American idea that some people are destined to rule the rest has never died. While most Americans have long supported "government of the people, by the people, and for the people," a small but influential

---

[137] "John C. Calhoun," National Park Service, accessed December 10, 2025, https://www.nps.gov/people/john-c-calhoun.htm.

[138] Abraham Lincoln, "The Gettysburg Address," archived at Abraham Lincoln Online, November 19, 1863, https://www.abrahamlincolnonline.org/lincoln/speeches/gettysburg.htm.

[139] June 25–26, 2025—Napolitan News survey of 1,000 registered voters.

cohort has believed—and still believes—that government of elites and by unelected experts would be better *for* the people.

In the years after the Civil War, a young scholar gave that impulse a new voice. Woodrow Wilson—future Democratic president—shared both Hamilton's reverence for top-down systems and Calhoun's despicable racism. He was also the product of something new in American life: the modern research university and its postgraduate schools. In fact, he is the only US president to have received a PhD

As Laurence Veysey wrote in his classic 1965 study *The Emergence of the American University*, "The university is…the distinctive creation of Western Europe."[140] Before the late nineteenth century, most American colleges were different—closely tied to theological concerns, with roughly 90 percent of college presidents drawn from the clergy.[141]

That changed quickly. Reformers sought to separate American universities "from orthodox evangelical piety" and embraced "European intellectual forms."[142] Many of the movement's leaders studied in Germany or under German-trained professors and set out to build American institutions on that model. The result was a new pipeline of credentialed expertise—an academic culture that would increasingly argue for governing through administration rather than with the consent of ordinary citizens.

Woodrow Wilson was part of this movement. He did his graduate work at Johns Hopkins, a university "founded in 1876 for the express purpose of bringing the German educational model to the

[140] Laurence R. Veysey, *The Emergency of the American University* (University of Chicago Press: 1970), 2.

[141] Ibid., 7.

[142] Ibid., 2.

United States."[143] His two closest teachers at Hopkins were Richard T. Ely and Herbert Baxter Adams, both of whom had earned their doctorates at Heidelberg University.

Ely, like Wilson, was horribly racist and a supporter of eugenics. He founded the American Economic Association (AEA) while Wilson was studying under him at Hopkins. The organization was strongly opposed to the American system of free-market economics; in fact, if you believed in free markets, you were not allowed to join.[144]

The German influence on Wilson's thinking is evident in "The Study of Administration," his influential 1887 article in *Political Science Quarterly*. As Hillsdale College professor Ronald J. Pestritto observed, "Wilson more or less urges the adoption of the Prussian administrative model in the United States."[145]

For Wilson and many of his academic colleagues, the problem with America is that voters are in charge. In "The Study of Administration," he lamented, "We have enthroned public opinion."[146] In his view, the sovereign people are "selfish, ignorant, timid, stubborn, or foolish."[147] If he were alive today, he might call them deplorable.

He preferred trained experts—"a corps of civil servants prepared by a special schooling and drilled, after appointment, into a perfect organization, with appropriate hierarchy and characteristic discipline."[148]

---

143 Ronald J. Pestritto, "The German Stamp on Wilson's Administrative Progressivism," *The American Mind*, The Claremont Institute, May 22, 2019, https://americanmind.org/salvo/the-german-stamp-on-wilsons-administrative-progressivism.

144 Robert Kirkby, "Dark Tales from the Early Days of the American Economic Association," personal blog, September 4, 2017, https://www.robertdkirkby.com/blog/2017/american-economic-association/.

145 Pestritto, "The German Stamp."

146 Woodrow Wilson, "The Study of Administration," in *Political Science Quarterly* 2, no. 2 (June 1887): 207.

147 Ibid., 208.

148 Ibid., 216.

Wilson would be pleased to know that half of America's policymaking and corporate elites today come from one of a dozen elite schools.[149]

He also favored an ever-expanding administrative state: specialists "seeing every day new things that the state ought to do." Once the experts decided what to do, "the next thing is to clearly see how it ought to do them."[150]

Wilson wanted elite rulers to lead voters, not follow them. Their role was to "make public opinion willing to listen and then see to it that it listens to the right thing. [They] must stir it up to search for an opinion, and then manage to put the right opinion in its way."[151] To paraphrase a Vietnam-era line, Wilson seemed to suggest that to save democracy, we had to destroy it.

With the backing of newly credentialed experts from the modern university system, Wilson helped turn progressive politics into an elitist revolt against America's founding ideals.

Unlike Hamilton or Calhoun, Wilson did not present his plan as a frontal assault on cherished principles. He insisted, with a straight face, that specially trained administrators would have nothing to do with politics. Voters would choose leaders to set policy; experts would simply make things work better.[152]

The Wilson blueprint has been unfolding for nearly a century and a half. Earlier elitists shared his views, but our twenty-eighth president built a mechanism to implement them. Bit by bit, new agencies and expert corps were added. Gradually, year after year, they assumed more authority.

The bureaucracy Wilson imagined shares his contempt for voters. A senior Health and Human Services official told professors Jennifer Bachner and Benjamin Ginsberg that "everyone knew" Washington

---

149 Thomas R. Dye, *Who's Running America*, 8th edition (Routledge: 2014).

150 Wilson, "The Study," 221.

151 Wilson, "The Study," 208.

152 The Study of Administration, p. 210

officialdom did not think much of the American people. In their view, "Many of the people are quite stupid, aren't they?"[153]

Bachner and Ginsberg also found that America's unelected officials "say it is more important to do what they think is right rather than to listen to the voice of the people."[154] They "favor a form of rule closer to the Confucian model, in which scholar-officials govern according to their own lights." And the public's role? "Ordinary people should respect authority and obey."[155]

Those un-American views would warm Woodrow Wilson's heart. If George Washington is the father of our country, Wilson might be seen as the father of the Elitist Revolt.

Voters have noticed. A Monmouth University poll found that 60 percent of Americans think "unelected or appointed government officials have too much influence in determining federal policy"—including 59 percent of Republicans, 59 percent of Democrats, and 62 percent of independents.[156]

That's not how America is supposed to work—but it is how Wilson and his progressive heirs designed the government to work. Today, voters recognize where this has led the nation: 60 percent believe the federal government has become a special-interest group that looks out primarily for its own interests. Only 23 percent disagree.[157]

We were closing in on the real enemy.

Before we trace how they sold these un-American ideas, a quick note on terminology. Wilson and his allies called themselves Progressives,

---

[153] Jennifer Bachner and Benjamin Ginsberg, *What Washington Gets Wrong* (Promethius: 2016), 9.

[154] Ibid., 108.

[155] Ibid., 115.

[156] "Public Troubled by 'Deep State'," Monmouth University, March 19, 2018, https://www.monmouth.edu/polling-institute/reports/monmouthpoll_us_031918/.

[157] January 27–28 2025—Napolitan News survey of 1,000 registered voters

but that label means something different today. To avoid confusion, I'll refer to them as Wilsonian Elitists. Likewise, while Administrative State accurately describes what Wilson wanted, it now carries partisan baggage. I'll use Wilsonian Government—or simply, government by the unelected.

Whatever we call it, my focus is the opposite of Wilson's. He treated popular sovereignty as a problem to overcome. I see it as a promise to keep and as the best hope for America's future.

In our 10/10/80 nation, many of the politically active 10 percent on both sides often share Wilson's temptation. They convince themselves the public is with them, discount America's founding ideals, and assume some people are destined to rule others. They'll say they're doing it "for the people." In reality, government by the unelected gets in the way of the people—and clears a path for their own policy goals and power.

Those who hold such views are the real enemy. They are loud, but small in number.

Our hope lies with the 80 percent who still embrace freedom, equality, and self-governance. They are the American majority—and the reason this fight can be won.

Chapter 7

THE RISE OF WILSONIAN GOVERNMENT

It is remarkable that Woodrow Wilson and his allies persuaded voters to cede so much authority to unelected bureaucrats. How they managed it offers lessons for anyone seeking to restore America's founding ideals.

One lesson is that politicians themselves are rarely as central as they imagine. Historians and political journalists often claim leaders set the national agenda, manage the economy, or single-handedly drive social change. That is mostly illusion. Real change usually begins far from official power.

Change begins with ordinary Americans adapting to the world around them—responding to new technologies, opportunities, economic disruptions, and shifting cultural norms. They are not consciously trying to bring about political change, but their choices reset the political environment.

Consider Ted Benna, a benefits consultant in King of Prussia, Pennsylvania. In 1978, he was frustrated that tax law favored the wealthy while doing little for middle-class families trying to save for retirement. That year Congress passed a modest bill trimming the top income-tax rate from 48 to 46 percent and reducing the effective capital-gains rate from 35 to 28 percent.[158] Nothing in the law explicitly aided retirement savings for average workers.

But Benna did something unusual in Washington—he read the statute closely. In paragraph 401(k), he spotted language that might allow ordinary workers to set aside tax-deferred savings. The provision was likely a drafting oversight, not an intentional policy. Yet Benna recognized its potential and refused to let it pass unnoticed. His persistence helped create what is now the backbone of American retirement security: the 401(k). Tens of millions of Americans today rely on accounts born from that accident.

A similar story of change beginning outside Washington came in 1869, when Wyoming granted women the right to vote. That breakthrough for the women's-suffrage movement didn't come from progressive ideals. It came from demographics. With six men for every woman in the territory, officials used suffrage as part of a marketing campaign to attract women to move there.

Congress, by contrast, waited another fifty years before granting women the vote nationwide. By then, about twenty states had already acted. In the end, Congress only ratified a reality shaped long before in the states—then claimed credit for it.

Both the 401(k) story and the suffrage story reveal the same pattern: Congress lagging behind the country. That is the norm in America's broken political system, where lawmakers often miss—or dismiss—what the public is already demanding.

In 2024, for example, voters overwhelmingly cared about two issues—the economy and border security. Nothing else came close. Yet the Elite One Percent and federal-government managers downplayed those concerns, focusing instead on guns, crime, health care, and climate change.[159]

---

[158] Rasmussen, Scott W., *The Sun Is Still Rising* (Sutherland Institute: 2018), p. 25.

[159] Napolitan Institute, "The Resistance," p.8

Many elites went further, mocking economic worries as silly. They were doing fine themselves, and government statistics suggested conditions were improving. From their perspective, the problem was not the economy—it was the voters.

But the official economic numbers—compiled by the government—never told the full story. They failed to capture the anxiety of families who felt they were falling behind. As Election Day approached, only 37 percent of voters thought they were better off than four years earlier. A mere 23 percent said their finances were improving, while 38 percent said the opposite—things were getting worse.[160]

To most Americans, the economy and the border were the only issues that mattered. To the Political Class, those concerns were annoying distractions from the agenda they wanted to impose.

Whenever such gaps appear between the governed and the governing, savvy leaders emerge to close them. They sense the mood, give voice to voter concerns, and shake up the political system until it catches up. Their role is less about setting an agenda than forcing the political world to hear what the public is already saying.

Many in the political world credit—or blame—Ronald Reagan for creating the tax revolt of the 1980s. In reality, the revolt was already well underway long before he became president. Middle-income Americans had been complaining about "bracket creep" for years as inflation pushed them into higher and higher tax brackets. In 1978, Congress cut rates in the same bill Ted Benna studied, and California voters approved Proposition 13, a sweeping tax-cutting initiative. The movement had momentum.

The revolt rattled leaders in both parties. Reagan, however, instinctively grasped the public mood and rode that wave all the way to the White House. His gift was giving voice to what Americans had already decided—and helping the political system catch up.

---

[160] Sept 9–10, 2024—Napolitan Institute survey of 1,000 registered voters.

Looking further back, many Americans mistakenly believe Thomas Jefferson's words in the Declaration of Independence inspired colonists to rise up and win their freedom. The history is less romantic. The colonists were first stirred to anger eleven years earlier by the Stamp Act.

What followed was a series of tense encounters that often fade from memory: the Townshend Acts, the Boston Massacre, the Intolerable Acts, the Boston Tea Party, and finally the creation of the Continental Congress. By 1774, tensions had boiled over, and on April 19, 1775, the shooting began at Lexington and Concord.

Fifteen months later, Jefferson seized the moment and drafted the timeless words that anchor our national heritage. By then, all but one of the British governors had already fled.[161] The fighting was underway, and the colonies were well along the path to independence.

Jefferson's words mattered, but they did not provoke a revolution. They captured and elevated the public mood. Later in life, Jefferson admitted as much: "It was intended to be an expression of the American mind, and to give to that expression the proper tone and spirit called for by the occasion."[162]

The Declaration gave clarity to what the colonies were fighting for and sustained morale through five more years of war. Like Reagan, Jefferson gave voice to a movement already in motion and rode it into history.

This does not diminish either man. Both rose to the occasion and played indispensable roles. But the movements that carried them forward began long before they appeared—and endured long after they were gone.

These are not isolated examples. They reflect the American norm: The people lead, and government lags behind. That same perspective

---

[161] Kevin P. Phillips, *The Cousins' Wars* (Harpercollins: 2000).

[162] Jefferson letter to Henry Lee, May 8, 2025. https://founders.archives.gov/documents/Jefferson/98-01-02-5212.

helps explain Woodrow Wilson's rise in the late nineteenth century. He sensed an opening for an elitist revolt amid the turbulence of his era.

Wilson was just thirty when he wrote *The Study of Administration.* By then, the country had endured a brutal Civil War. Two presidents had already been assassinated in his lifetime, and a third would soon follow. Three presidential assassinations in thirty-six years gave a vivid sense of how unsettled American society was.

The war's aftermath was only part of the upheaval. Gas lamps were spreading across the continent, transforming daily life. That may not sound revolutionary to people in the digital age, but for millennia darkness fell with the sun. Then came Edison's electric light bulb—patented just two years after Wilson's treatise—hinting at still greater change to come.

The pace of transformation was staggering. The first oil well opened in Titusville, Pennsylvania, when Wilson was a toddler. Rockefeller's Standard Oil rose during his youth.[163, 164] At twelve, he watched the nation linked by a transcontinental railroad, while the telegraph made communication possible in ways never imagined. The Industrial Revolution advanced at breakneck speed, accompanied by the rise of giant corporate monopolies.

These changes, layered on top of the Civil War, reshaped not just society but the perception of the country itself. America felt less like a loose collection of states and more like a single, unified nation.

At the same time, all this change left many with the uneasy sense that their fate was being shaped by distant powers. Farmers in the

---

[163] "The U.S. petroleum industry began in 1859 to meet demand for 'Coal Oil' — the popular lamp fuel kerosene," AOGHS, accessed December 10, 2025, https://aoghs.org/petroleum-pioneers/american-oil-history/.

[164] "A History of John D. Rockefeller's Standard Oil," Fuel Express, November 14, 2017, https://www.fuelexpress.net/blog/general-information/history-john-d-rockefellers-standard-oil/.

West understood when weather cut into their income. But after the Civil War, outside forces seemed to control their finances.

John Deere's first plow in 1837 made farming easier and opened the Midwest prairie to cultivation. After the war, sales soared—and so did production. More crops, though, meant lower prices. Railroads expanded markets for selling the crops, but many suspected monopolies weren't playing fair.

In response, a broad Populist Movement took root. It was more than politics; it was a cultural phenomenon. Farmers across the South and Midwest built alliances in new ways. Hatred of elites ran so deep that outlaw Jesse James was hailed by some as a folk hero. Nearly a century later, a television series even portrayed him as a farmer driven to crime after the railroads killed his mother.

Populist imagery seeped into popular culture. Some believe *The Wizard of Oz* carried hidden meaning: The witches symbolized farmers' two great enemies—mortgage bankers and drought. One died under a falling house, the other by water. The Scarecrow and Tin Man embodied the alliance between farmers and factory workers. In L. Frank Baum's original book, Dorothy's slippers were silver, not ruby—walking on the yellow brick road to symbolize the demand for money backed by both silver and gold. It was an emotionally charged issue at the time. The 1896 Democratic nominee, William Jennings Bryan, captured it with his thunderous line: "You shall not crucify mankind upon a cross of gold."[165]

Farmers were angry, anxious, and searching for someone to blame.

Into this volatility stepped Wilson and other young academics. They believed the chaos could be contained only through the "science

[165] Harvey Ellsworth Newbranch, "William Jennings Bryan: A Concise But Complete Story of His Life and Services" (The University Publishing Co.: 1900).

of administration."[166] In their view, voters were the problem and experts the solution. They embraced government by the unelected.

By the late nineteenth century, support for rule by "experts" and distrust of voters had grown steadily among influential leaders. Some saw America's experiment in self-governance as a temporary deviation from 2,500 years of political philosophy that treated popular rule as absurd. Others feared the Populist movement outright. Still others simply assumed they were destined to rule.

There was also another, less savory reason many Wilsonian Elitists wanted to limit the influence of voters.

After the Civil War, Black Americans won the right to vote. In fact, two Black men served in the US Senate and fourteen in the House of Representatives. Hundreds of other formerly disenfranchised Black citizens were elected to state legislatures and local governing bodies.[167] Pathetically, Jim Crow laws and state-backed repression soon stripped away those rights.

Still, the fact that it had happened at all was something the racists would not forget.

Wilson himself was deeply racist, as were many leaders in the defeated South (and not only in the South). In the eyes of many elitists, the expansion of voting rights was alarming. Particularly offensive to some was that a Black senator, Hiram Revels, took the Mississippi seat previously held by Jefferson Davis—once a hero to the racists for serving as president of the Confederate rebellion.[168]

Adding to what the elitists saw as a problem, several new territories were allowing women to vote, and the suffrage movement was gaining momentum. Wilson and many of his allies were strongly opposed to women's suffrage.

---

[166] Wilson, "The Study."

[167] History.com Editors, "Black Leaders During Reconstruction," History.com, last updated May 28, 2025, https://www.history.com/articles/black-leaders-during-reconstruction.

[168] Ibid.

Whatever their reasons, these elitists shared a conviction: Wilsonian Government was the solution, and voters were the problem. For them, the prospect of Blacks and women voting only magnified the danger. Wilson called "popular sovereignty" the greatest threat to enlightened government.[169]

Blaming voters for America's ills resonated with nineteenth-century elitists much as "No taxation without representation" had once rallied colonial Americans. Their challenge was how to sell that message in a populist era.

That's where Wilson came in. He gave voice to the elitist revolt by providing a softer language. Instead of sounding like Hamilton or Calhoun, he insisted administration had nothing to do with politics. Voters, he claimed, were still in charge. The only question was whether complex decisions should be made by professional, nonpartisan experts—or by a petty, dysfunctional Congress.

Talk about an easy sell.

Given a choice between Congress and almost anything else, voters would usually choose the alternative. Even today, only 31 percent of Americans say their own representative is the best person for the job—and their view of Congress as a whole is far worse.[170]

Armed with this logic, Wilson and his allies were ready to harness public discontent. In 1887—the same year Wilson published *The Study of Administration*—Congress created the Interstate Commerce Commission (ICC), the nation's first independent regulatory agency. It was established "in response to charges that farmers and merchants were being forced to pay exorbitant railroad rates to ship their products to market."[171]

---

169 Wilson, "The Study."

170 July 6–8, 2022—Napolitan News survey of 1,000 registered voters.

171 "A Brief History of Administrative Government," Center for Effective Government, accessed December 10, 2025, https://www.foreffectivegov.org/node/3461.

Elitists acknowledged populist concerns, validated them, and then prescribed their cure: more power for unelected officials. Like a hammer looking for a nail, their answer was always more bureaucracy. And to a frustrated public, weary of being ignored, at least it looked like someone was offering solutions.

But the outcome was predictable. Corruption soon followed.

As the Center for Effective Government later observed, "It was not long before many 'independent' regulatory commissions were being accused of being 'captives' of the industries they were supposed to regulate." Sometimes the industries even backed the commissions themselves—as a way to eliminate competition and lock in profits. Corporations learned quickly that cozying up to regulators was good business.[172]

It's worth noting how well Wilson's framing positioned the elitists. Corruption and cronyism plagued the ICC, but would Congress have done better? At least, in the eyes of "reformers," Wilson and his allies had acted.

Like many true believers in utopian fantasies, Wilson reached for a familiar excuse when things didn't work out as planned: He claimed that the reforms didn't work because they hadn't gone far enough. We never really gave them a fair try.

His real hope was more ambitious. He urged the United States to "follow the lead of the governments of Europe in buying or building both telegraph and railroad lines."[173] In his view, whatever the private sector could do, government could do better. With a straight face, he even cited the "utility, cheapness, and success of the government's postal service" as proof the government should also seize "control of the telegraph system."[174]

---

[172] Ibid.

[173] Wilson, "The Study."

[174] Ibid.

From that perspective, the ICC was only a baby step. Any failures were blamed on private companies still being in the mix. The obvious solution—to Wilson—was to push the private sector aside and let government run the railroads outright.

Despite the ICC's corruption, Wilsonian Elitists pressed ahead with their dream of government by the unelected. In the decades that followed, regulatory agencies multiplied, and by the twentieth century, the model was entrenched.

Those of us who deplore what Wilson and his allies accomplished can still learn from the way they persuaded voters to surrender so much power.

First, Wilson and his allies knew exactly what they wanted and how to talk about it. They were true believers in government by "experts," and they cast popular sovereignty as the real enemy.

We must have the same clarity. *Government by the unelected* is the enemy. Restoring power to voters is the solution.

Second, the Elitists didn't waste time debating theories of government. They spoke to real concerns and offered what they claimed were solutions. In a theoretical debate, Populists and Elitists would have been miles apart. But when Elitists promised answers to problems Populists cared about, differences blurred.

We must do the same. People facing real struggles don't want abstract debates; they want solutions. We don't need to convince everyone of the dangers of Wilsonian Elitists. We need to show how America's founding ideals still solve twenty-first-century problems.

Finally, Wilson and his allies were persistent. They were patient and seized every opportunity to expand the reach of unelected officials. In today's language, they never let a crisis go to waste.

Wilson was elected president twenty-five years after publishing his landmark article. Once in office, he pressed ahead with the same agenda. As a young academic, he had called for the nation to buy or build "both telegraph and railroad lines."[175] As president, he went further—nationalizing the railroads, the telegraph companies, and the phone company.

As president, Wilson also continued to display his utter contempt for the views of those he sought to govern. He campaigned for re-election on a promise to keep the nation out of World War I and then asked for a Declaration of War within a month of taking office.

When the nation didn't respond as he wished, he instituted a military draft. But, in language that would make George Orwell blush, Wilson declared that the draft was "in no sense a conscription of the unwilling." As he saw it, it was nothing more than a "selection from a Nation which has volunteered in mass."[176]

The Wilsonian Government by the Unelected has been taking shape for nearly 140 years. It will not be dismantled overnight. But if it took patience and persistence to build, it will take the same to tear down.

---

[175] Ibid.

[176] Woodrow Wilson, May 19, 1917, Message Regarding Military Draft, https://millercenter.org/the-presidency/presidential-speeches/may-19-1917-message-regarding-military-draft

Chapter 8

THE GREAT TURNAROUND

The twentieth century was an age of astonishing growth and transformation. When it began, the average American could expect to live just forty-seven years. By century's end, life expectancy had climbed to seventy-seven.[177]

At the close of the nineteenth century, bicycles represented the cutting edge of transportation. Orville and Wilbur Wright—drawing on skills from their bicycle shop—soon launched the first successful airplane. Within a few decades, the world had gone from bicycles to automobiles, from automobiles to jets, and eventually to landing men on the moon.

The pace of change touched every corner of daily life. In 1900, hardly any American homes had electricity; by 2000, life without it was unimaginable. Fewer than 1 percent of Americans had telephones at the dawn of the century. By mid-century, landlines were nearly universal. By century's end, they were already becoming relics.[178]

---

[177] Elizabeth Arias et al., "United States Life Tables, 2021," in *National Vital Statistics Reports* 72, no. 12 (November 7, 2023), https://www.cdc.gov/nchs/data/nvsr/nvsr72/nvsr72-12.pdf.

[178] "1870s–1940s: Telephone," Elon University, accessed December 10, 2025, https://www.elon.edu/u/imagining/time-capsule/150-years/back-1870-1940/#past-predictions.

The shock of such change is hard to fathom. President Rutherford B. Hayes, upon seeing the telephone for the first time, reportedly told Alexander Graham Bell: "That's an amazing invention, but who would ever want to use one of them?"[179]

Yet not all change was welcome. The twentieth century also brought two devastating world wars, the Great Depression, systemic efforts by government to deny Black Americans their newly won freedoms, and other tragedies.

The upheaval of the early twentieth century gave Woodrow Wilson's vision of government by the unelected new momentum. As businesses, banks, and cities expanded and became more centralized, it seemed natural that American politics and government should go with the flow and expand in parallel.

At the dawn of the twentieth century, federal spending accounted for just 2 percent of the nation's GDP. Generally speaking, what happened in Washington had little impact on the day-to-day lives of everyday Americans. By century's end, the presence of federal rules and regulations was unavoidable as federal spending rose to nearly one out of every five dollars spent in America—and the trajectory pointed upward into the twenty-first century.[180]

This shift carried profound consequences. In the 1940s, for the first time, federal spending exceeded that of all state and local governments combined. That imbalance never reversed. States, once the primary engines of governance, were reduced to subordinate offices of Washington's bureaucracy. The result was a steady reordering of power—away from local self-governance and toward a centralized national authority.

---

[179] Ibid.

[180] "Budget FY 2025 - Historical Tables, Budget of the United States Government, Fiscal Year 2025," Gov Info, accessed December 10, 2025, https://www.govinfo.gov/app/details/BUDGET-2025-TAB/context.

Second, financing the federal government's expansion required new revenue streams. The income tax was introduced, and payroll taxes soon followed. Before the twentieth century, the Constitution barred Washington from taxing citizens directly. The Sixteenth Amendment changed that, creating the federal income tax and permanently altering the relationship between Americans and their government.

One other societal change proved pivotal in sustaining Wilson's vision: the rise of mass media. The early twentieth century witnessed the growth of national newspaper chains and wire services. By then, virtually all White Americans could read and write, creating a truly mass audience. Illiteracy among Black Americans remained high—a problem largely ignored by the political and media elite.

With national outlets shaping the news, Americans across regions and classes increasingly encountered the same stories and the same narratives. Radio in the 1920s and television a few decades later only amplified that reach, consolidating control of public opinion in the hands of a few national outlets.

The explosion of mass media shaped how Americans experienced the twentieth century—and the world in which the two Midwestern women grew up. It created a national storehouse of shared memories: Franklin D. Roosevelt's reassurance that "the only thing we have to fear is fear itself," the assassination of John F. Kennedy, antiwar protests, and Martin Luther King Jr.'s unforgettable "I Have a Dream" speech.

The shared culture extended far beyond politics: the Beatles on *The Ed Sullivan Show*, the rise of the Super Bowl, the *Star Wars* saga, and perhaps the single most-watched event in human history—Neil Armstrong's first step on the moon. "That's one small step for a man, one giant leap for mankind."

This new media environment was ideal for those who sought government by the unelected. A handful of editors and producers could decide what counted as news and how it should be framed.

They leaned heavily on government officials as authoritative sources. This was precisely what Wilson had envisioned in his 1887 article: specially trained experts ensuring the public "listens to the right things." In his view, elites would set the agenda for everyone else.[181]

For Wilson, it was not only about controlling the agenda but also about shaping public opinion itself. He believed the role of elites was to guide people to "search for an opinion" on the topics they chose to highlight. Once the public had been drawn into that process, the final step was for government officials "to put the right opinion in its way."[182]

Looking back, it is chilling to see how completely Wilson's vision came to life. A handful of media gatekeepers held a monopoly on setting the national agenda and defining what counted as news. By the 1970s, 95 percent of Americans tuned in to one of three national television networks during prime time.[183] News was whatever Walter Cronkite—or Chet Huntley and David Brinkley—told the country it was. Different anchors, but essentially the same script. Much of what aired was little more than a televised summary of that morning's *The New York Times*.

If a story made it into the twenty-two minutes of national news programming each night, it became part of the nation's collective reality. Stories left out—no matter how significant—might as well not have existed.

When presidents spoke to the nation, every other television program went dark. If you turned on the TV, you watched the Oval Office address—there was no alternative. Half of all American households tuned in as Richard Nixon or Jimmy Carter spoke directly to them.

---

181 Wilson, "The Study," 208.

182 Ibid.

183 "Issues and Trends in the Television Industry," Media and Culture, Lumen Learning, accessed December 10, 2025, https://courses.lumenlearning.com/suny-hccc-massmedia/chapter/9-3-issues-and-trends-in-the-television-industry.

To twenty-first-century ears, it may sound unbelievable: The opposing party wasn't even granted the courtesy of a televised rebuttal.

In that environment, persuasion didn't require brilliance. You could sell your agenda simply by speaking to half the nation unopposed. And with a team of White House speechwriters scripting the words, the message was carefully managed from start to finish.

Still, elite control never quite reached the totalitarian levels imagined by George Orwell in *1984*. Not everyone read the front page or even glanced at the headlines. Many Americans turned first to the sports scores, local news, or the comics. My own first memory of reading "news" was a story about the drummer in a new band—Ringo Starr's real name was Richard Starkey.

Another check on elite control came from Americans who exercised what political scientist Albert O. Hirschman called the right to "exit" rather than follow the prescribed narrative. "The movement of groups like the hippies is very much in the American tradition," he observed. They were branded un-American by some, but in typical American fashion they chose "flight rather than fight." Instead of trying to repair a system they saw as broken, they created a separate "scene."[184]

Even so, media control of the national agenda was about as complete as it could be for champions of top-down government. Free speech was easy for elites to celebrate because the gatekeepers shared their assumptions. Views they considered dangerous rarely reached the public. Those voices were denied a platform and, for all practical purposes, silenced.

At times, however, centralized media power served a noble purpose. Coverage of the civil rights movement forced Americans outside the South to confront what Jim Crow society truly looked like. That changed everything. Without the glare of national television,

---

[184] Albert O. Hirschman, *Exit, Voice, and Loyalty* (Harvard University Press: 1970), 108.

the movement might never have brought the country closer to fulfilling its founding ideals.

Centralized power also enabled one of America's most extraordinary achievements—NASA's project to land a man on the moon and return him safely to Earth. As a child, I followed the program with awe from beginning to end.

But the same concentration of authority had a darker side. An elite consensus that shut out dissent produced one of the greatest debacles in American history: the Vietnam War. As David Halberstam documented in *The Best and the Brightest*, the era's most celebrated minds fundamentally misunderstood the conflict. Their failure sent 58,220 young Americans to their deaths—along with millions of people across Vietnam, Cambodia, and Laos.[185] It was a war that should never have been fought.

I have great respect for all who did their duty and fought with honor in Vietnam. But like many in my generation, I carry a deep resentment toward the leaders who sent them to fight. I remain embarrassed by how Vietnam veterans were treated when they returned home. The same leaders who sent them into war without a plan to win failed to stand by them afterward. They should have honored those they sent into battle. Instead, in the elite world, those soldiers mattered little—and so they were abandoned.

Centralized media control also played a crucial role in enabling the disaster. In 1964, President Johnson falsely claimed that North Vietnamese patrol boats had launched an unprovoked attack on US naval destroyers. The press repeated the story and rallied support for the Gulf of Tonkin Resolution. Only years later did reporters begin

---

[185] "American War and Military Operations Casualties: Lists and Statistics," Congressional Research Service, updated July 29, 2020, https://web.archive.org/web/20230514171012if_/https://sgp.fas.org/crs/natsec/RL32492.pdf.

to acknowledge that Johnson had misled the nation about what happened in the Tonkin Gulf.[186]

By then it was too late. The congressional resolution gave the president legal authority to escalate a war he had already chosen to fight. The fabricated attacks by patrol boats served only as an excuse.

Through it all, the 1960s economy kept booming as it had since the end of World War II. The postwar recovery had stunned the nation. When the war ended, many economists and ordinary Americans expected a return to depression. Instead, the country entered an era of unprecedented prosperity. Government economists quickly claimed credit, insisting they had learned how to "fine-tune" the economy.[187]

A more accurate assessment would have been that earlier government policies had created and prolonged the Depression. After World War II, America was the world's only intact industrial power, and postwar economists didn't repeat the mistakes of the Depression era. That allowed the economy to flourish. The good times sustained popular confidence in government and support for the status quo. If Washington could win the war, it seemed, surely it could win the peace.

By the 1960s, government by unelected officials had become a dominant feature of American life. Over a century of expansion, the bureaucracy had entrenched itself in every sphere of public life. Because the economy appeared strong, more than 70 percent of voters trusted Washington to do the right thing most of the time.[188] As the

---

186 "Tonkin Gulf Resolution," Eighty-eighth Congress of the United States of America, archived at Archives.gov, January 7, 1964, https://www.archives.gov/milestone-documents/tonkin-gulf-resolution.

187 Phillip Cagan et al., *Economic Policy and Inflation in the Sixties* (The American Enterprise Institute: 1972).

188 "Public Trust in Government: 1958-2025," Pew Research Center, December 4, 2025, https://www.pewresearch.org/politics/2025/12/04/public-trust-in-government-1958-2025/.

1960s gave way to the 1970s and 1980s, elites naturally assumed that expert rule was the permanent order of things. Why wouldn't it be?

John Kenneth Galbraith, one of the most prominent economists of the era, argued that the economies of the United States and the Soviet Union would ultimately converge. Capitalist or socialist, both would be steered by a "managerial" class of experts.[189]

Galbraith's views echoed those of Richard Ely, Woodrow Wilson's mentor. Both dismissed the idea that free markets could outperform government-directed economies. Galbraith's confidence in the Soviet model ran so deep that as late as 1984—on the eve of its collapse—he praised its "great material progress" and claimed it used its manpower more efficiently than the United States.[190]

Anchored in his faith in the managerial class and top-down government, Galbraith assumed the age of entrepreneurial innovation was over. "The large business organization," he wrote, "alone can deploy the requisite capital; it alone can mobilize the requisite skills."[191] He and his peers were so enamored with large institutions run by managers that they overlooked what was happening beneath the surface. As Galbraith put it, "There is no case that such innovation will come better from the little man."[192]

At that very moment, entrepreneurs and start-ups were discovering how technologies spun off from the space race could launch an entirely new communications era. That revolution would soon turn the world Galbraith knew upside down—and pose an existential threat to Wilsonian Government.

One of the most important breakthroughs was the deployment of communications satellites. Without any thought of politics, I

---

[189] John Kenneth Galbraith, *The New Industrial State* (Princeton University Press: 2007).

[190] Galbraith, August 27, 1984, New Yorker, *A Visit to Russia.*

[191] Galbraith, *Industrial State*, 40.

[192] Ibid.

found myself playing a small part in transforming this technology into a direct challenge to the established order.

In 1978, my father and I planned to provide television programming for Connecticut cable systems. We expected to deliver shows the standard way—through AT&T landlines. Then, through a series of unplanned encounters, we discovered satellite broadcasting. That discovery changed everything. Suddenly, we could beam programming nationwide for less money than it cost to send the same shows across Connecticut by landline.

Building on that breakthrough, we launched ESPN on September 7, 1979. CNN followed the next year, then MTV and many other cable networks.

Why did this threaten Wilson's dream? Because cable gave Americans a choice. If they didn't want to watch the network news, they could turn to sports, music, movies—or something else entirely. Cable shattered the monopoly elites had enjoyed over public opinion.

By 1979, the three major television networks—ABC, NBC, and CBS—were watched by about 40 percent of households on a typical night.[193] And for the most part, they told the same story. Today, those networks barely reach 14 percent of households.[194] Even adding cable news, the combined total is less than 20 percent—just half of what it was when ESPN first went on the air.[195]

Once viewers had alternatives, presidents lost their ability to speak directly to half the nation. As more people tuned out, the

---

[193] Les Brown, "Audiences for TV Newscasts in Dramatic Increase," *The New York Times*, December 3, 1979, https://timesmachine.nytimes.com/timesmachine/1979/12/03/111123977.html?pageNumber=53.

[194] Mark Mwachiro, "Here Are the Evening News Ratings for the 2024-2025 TV Season," *Adweek*, September 23, 2025, https://www.adweek.com/tvnewser/here-are-the-evening-news-ratings-for-the-2024-2025-tv-season/.

[195] Mark Mwachiro, "Week of Sept. 29 Cable News Ratings: Cable Nets See Gains in Total Viewers," *Adweek*, October 9, 2025, https://www.adweek.com/tvnewser/week-of-september-29-2025-cable-news-ratings/.

divide widened between those inside the political bubble and the rest of America. In Washington, everyone still parsed presidential speeches. In much of the country, people often didn't even know the president had spoken.

The 1980 debate between Ronald Reagan and Jimmy Carter drew 93 percent of voters.[196] It was a national moment, witnessed by activists, undecideds, and millions in between. By 2024, however, only hardened partisans tuned in to the Trump–Harris debate. Fewer than 1 percent of viewers were undecided, and most could not fathom how anyone could support the other side.[197]

That 1980 debate gave voters a real chance to evaluate the candidates and their positions. Today, presidential debates no longer serve that purpose. They resemble college football rivalries instead. Viewers are not watching to decide—they are there to cheer for their team.

The end result was that three television networks, clustered just a few blocks apart in New York City, could no longer dictate what counted as news. The splintering of audiences meant the gatekeepers were losing their grip. As former CIA analyst Martin Gurri observed, "A revolution in the nature and content of communication…has ended the top-down control elites exerted on the public during the industrial age."[198]

It was one thing to give people the option of ignoring what elites deemed important. What came next was even more devastating for believers in Wilsonian Government. Personal computers arrived in

---

[196] Highest Rated Presidential Debates, 1960 to present, https://www.nielsen.com/insights/2008/top-ten-presidential-debates-1960-to-present/

[197] "Overwhelming Majority of Voters Can't Understand Why You'd Vote for the Other Candidate," Napolitan News Service, October 12, 2024, https://napolitannews.org/posts/overwhelming-majority-of-voters-cant-understand-why-youd-vote-for-the-other-candidate.

[198] Martin Gurri, *The Revolt of the Public and the Crisis of Authority in the New Millennium* (Stripe Press: 2018), 65.

the 1980s and the Internet in the 1990s. Suddenly, there were no gatekeepers. Anyone could become a publisher.

The scale of new content creation is almost beyond comprehension. One study found that "more information was generated in 2001 than in all the previous existence of our species on Earth."[199] In a single year, more content was created than in all the centuries of elite media control, from the printing press to network TV. Then the explosion accelerated: the total amount of information doubled in 2002, doubled again in 2003, and has never slowed since.[200]

For content creators, the equation had changed completely. In the old era, gatekeepers controlled both the platform and the audience. You had to play by their rules. To appear on *The Ed Sullivan Show*, the Rolling Stones were forced to change the lyrics of one of their hit songs. Sullivan thought the original words were inappropriate. The band had no choice but to comply—because Sullivan had the audience.

In the new era, anyone could publish. It no longer mattered whether Ed Sullivan liked your lyrics or Walter Cronkite approved of your perspective. The gatekeepers were gone. Technically, anyone's content could be seen by almost anyone else, anywhere in the world. The challenge was no longer access—it was how to capture attention and keep it.

Galbraith and his peers were slow to grasp what was happening. Others saw it clearly. In *The End of Big*, Nicco Mele explained: "The devices and connectivity so essential to modern life put unprecedented power in the hands of every individual—a radical redistribution of power that our traditional institutions don't and perhaps can't understand."[201]

---

[199] Ibid., 20.

[200] Ibid.

[201] Nicco Mele, *The End of Big* (Picador: 2014).

In the 1990s, I tried to build my polling brand by offering free local polls to newspapers. All they had to do was give me credit in print and provide a link to my site online. I was told in no uncertain terms that local newspapers would never—*never*—link to another website. They had the brand. They were the source people trusted for news.

Today, local newspapers are on life support. Their legacy brand is no match for a world where anyone can publish without permission. As Nicco Mele put it, "Radical connectivity is toxic to conventional power structures."[202]

Cable had already given Americans a choice, breaking the elites' grip on the national agenda. Now the internet demolished their ability to restrict the flow of ideas altogether. People could publish contrarian views instantly, without anyone's approval. Suddenly, the public could talk back. Political leaders could issue a statement—and ordinary citizens could reply on the very same platform. Woodrow Wilson would be horrified.

At first, legacy media outlets dismissed it all. They mocked the quality of online content, laughed at the small audiences, and questioned the credibility of anyone presenting a different perspective.

They're not laughing anymore. Without permission from anyone, a podcaster like Joe Rogan can reach a bigger audience than CNN or MSNBC. To get a sense of just how much these alternative voices can change the national conversation, imagine how Americans would have responded to Wilson's claim that the military draft was "in no sense a conscription of the unwilling."

Perhaps the most dramatic example of the change is the career path of Bari Weiss. In 2020, she resigned from *The New York Times*, a publication that during the 1960s and '70s was the premier gatekeeper for the elitist narrative. In an earlier time, that would have been the end of her career. Instead, after departing from the *Times*,

[202] Ibid.

Weiss launched a Substack newsletter that blossomed into an online media company.

While legacy media outlets struggled, Weiss attracted 1.5 million subscribers and built a powerful *The Free Press* brand. Just five years after leaving the *Times*, Weiss sold her new media company to the once-mighty CBS for $150 million and became editor in chief of CBS News. In a very real sense, Bari Weiss personified how the new media outlets defeated the elitist gatekeepers of the legacy press.[203]

Under the guidance of Weiss, the network was forced to admit that legacy media had lost the trust of the American people. One reason is that it had previously paid too much attention to advocates, academics and elites rather than average Americans.[204]

Having to deal with the new platforms giving voice to average Americans, the legacy media lost the ability to bury inconvenient stories. When a Ukrainian refugee was murdered in Charlotte in a brutal, unprovoked attack, there was virtually no national coverage at first. But once the story began trending on X, the gatekeepers couldn't contain it. From that point on, nearly every outlet was forced to cover the tragic story of Iryna Zarutska.[205]

In short, by the 1970s our society had begun a Great Turnaround. For all of American history up to that point, nearly every institution had been growing larger, more centralized, and more homogenized. That trajectory empowered top-down government and Politically Active Elites.

---

[203] Rachel Treisman, "Who is Bari Weiss? CBS News' new editor-in-chief is a vocal critic of legacy media," NPR, October 6, 2025, https://www.npr.org/2025/10/06/nx-s1-5563786/bari-weiss-cbs-news-free-press.

[204] Caroline Vakil, *New 'CBS Evening News' anchor pledges transparency, urges viewers to hold him accountable,* The Hill, January 1, 2026 https://thehill.com/blogs/pundits-blog/media/5669062-tony-dokoupil-cbs-evening-news/

[205] Robby Soave, "Media finally notices brutal Iryna Zarutska murder, blames MAGA for caring," *The Hill,* September 9, 2025, https://thehill.com/opinion/robbys-radar/5494025-iryna-zarutska-stabbing-charlotte/.

But beginning in the 1970s, everything reversed. Over the past half century, society has grown ever more decentralized and customized. That shift allowed new voices to be heard—voices from people whose lives do not revolve around politics or government. Adding these voices to the national dialogue revealed views that elitists had long tried to ignore or suppress.

Populists regarded self-reliance as the essence of democracy. As Christopher Lasch observed, it was "a virtue that never went out of demand." They resisted efforts to make everything about politics and government, which they believed "weakened the spirit of self-reliance and discouraged people from taking responsibility for their actions."[206]

Such perspectives were ignored when elite gatekeepers controlled the agenda. These mainstream perspectives reflected a sharp contrast to the elite vision of America: "Democracy works best when men and women do things for themselves, with the help of their friends and neighbors, instead of depending on the state." As Lasch emphasized, this was not nostalgia for rugged individualism. It was an affirmation that self-governing communities—not isolated individuals—are the foundation of a democratic society.[207]

The most profound impact of the Great Turnaround is that elites can no longer exclude such voices from the national dialogue. In a decentralizing society, defenders of government by the unelected have already lost. They cannot win in the court of public opinion.

Simply put, a centralized, top-down government cannot survive in a decentralizing, bottom-up society. The era of Wilsonian Government is over; the Wilsonian Elitists just don't know it yet.

---

[206] Lasch, *Revolt*, 83.
[207] Ibid., 7.

Chapter 9

A PERFECT STORM

Born in the 1960s, the two Midwestern women grew up simply assuming they would go to college. They had no idea that this expectation itself marked a major shift in American society.

At the start of the 1960s, college was still a rare and elite experience. Fewer than 7 percent of American adults held a degree.[208] Even more striking to twenty-first-century Americans, more than 25 US senators lacked a college degree, and over one hundred members of the House of Representatives had never graduated.[209]

Today the picture is radically different. Nearly 14 percent of Americans hold a postgraduate degree—meaning Americans are now twice as likely to have an advanced degree as they were in 1960 to

---

208 "1960 Census: Population, Supplementary Reports: Educational Attainment of the Population of the United States," US Census Bureau, December 27, 1962, https://www.census.gov/library/publications/1962/dec/population-pc-s1-37.html.

209 Katherine Schaeffer, "Nearly all members of the 118th Congress have a bachelor's degree – and most have a graduate degree, too," Pew Research Center, February 2, 2023, https://www.pewresearch.org/short-reads/2023/02/02/nearly-all-members-of-the-118th-congress-have-a-bachelors-degree-and-most-have-a-graduate-degree-too/.

have a bachelor's.[210] In Congress, the transformation is even clearer: More senators today hold postgraduate degrees than the number who held bachelor's degrees in 1960. All senators, and nearly all House members, are now college graduates.[211]

The expectation that middle-class children would attend college emerged just as centralization in American society was reaching its peak. That shift helped set the stage for the political turmoil of the twenty-first century. To grasp its significance, it is essential to recognize how exclusive a college education was before the cultural upheavals of the 1960s.

Perhaps the most striking example is that, in 1960, two sitting US Supreme Court justices—Hugo Black and Charles Whittaker—had not even finished high school. To modern readers that seems unthinkable, but it reflected a reality in which only about 40 percent of American adults had earned a high school diploma.[212]

In those days, you didn't need a credential from a law school to take the bar exam and practice law. All you needed was the knowledge to pass the exam.

By the 1960s, the role of college in American life was rapidly changing. Today, the share of Americans with a college degree is about the same as the share with only a high school diploma in 1960. That surge was fueled by a symbiotic relationship between government and universities. The GI Bill of the 1940s encouraged millions of World War II veterans to pursue higher education, and by the 1960s the federal government was backing student loans.

By 1965, when historian Laurence Veysey published his study of the American university, it was clear that colleges had become central institutions in American life. What had once been an elite

---

210 "1960 Census."

211 Schaeffer, "Congress."

212 Robert Kominski et al., "We the Americans: Our Education," US Department of Commerce, September 1993, https://www2.census.gov/library/publications/decennial/1990/we-the-americans/we-11.pdf.

experience was increasingly shared by the middle class. Veysey and others observed that "the university may become as characteristic an institution in America as the church was 300 years ago."[213] It was a striking claim, given the church's dominant role in colonial America, but it fit the mood of the 1960s and '70s—peak years for centralized authority and elite control of the media narrative.

In that era, the idea that properly educated experts should run the country seemed as natural as the expectation that the two Midwestern girls would go to college. Universities eagerly embraced the *Wilsonian* vision, since their very business was certifying educated experts. A natural alliance formed among universities, the *Wilsonian Government,* and media gatekeepers.

Credentialed professors became indispensable—not only to staff the swelling ranks of government agencies but also to shape a media narrative congenial to America's elites. The academic world suddenly commanded vast influence over society.

By the mid-1960s, Veysey concluded that "the university in the United States had become largely an agency of social control." For an institution rooted in a German intellectual tradition skeptical of America's founding ideals, that was a remarkable achievement. Yet by 1965 Veysey could confidently declare that the "primary responsibility" of American universities was "the custodianship of popular values."[214]

The values universities were guarding were elite values. Still, in the early 60s, the gap between elites and the general public was not nearly as wide as it is today. At that time, the elites directing government and media still viewed America as a force for good in the world. In the wake of victory in World War II and the post-war economic boom, voters trusted government at levels never seen before—or since.

---

[213] Veysey, *American University*, x.

[214] Ibid., 240.

Few realized how fleeting that moment would be. As they gained power and influence, the universities did not remain neutral custodians of shared values. Instead, they began imposing new and alien values, inflicting profound damage on the nation.

On January 4, 1965, President Lyndon B. Johnson's State of the Union address laid out his ambitious Great Society agenda. These were heady days for champions of *Wilsonian Government* by the unelected. "Following Johnson's lead, Congress enacted sweeping legislation in the areas of civil rights, health care, education, and the environment."[215]

Many in academia embraced the Great Society as consistent with their "custodianship of popular values." This was the world long envisioned by Woodrow Wilson, John Kenneth Galbraith, and other elitists: Government would take responsibility for everything.

And, of course, many in the elite bubble recognized that LBJ's program would require more government "experts." It was an open invitation for elites to expand their influence and remake American society.

The rest of 1965 did not go according to plan. Within months of Johnson's speech, Malcolm X was assassinated, and other civil-rights leaders were murdered. On March 7, a group of Black Americans marching from Selma to Montgomery were brutally attacked at the Edmund Pettus Bridge in what became known as Bloody Sunday. They were demanding the right to vote. Thousands ultimately completed the fifty-four-mile march to the Alabama state capitol—but only under the protection of federal marshals and the National Guard.

The turmoil escalated. That summer, Los Angeles erupted in the Watts riots, which left several dozen dead and dominated newscasts.

---

[215] History.com editors, "L. B. J. envisions a Great Society in his State of the Union Address," History.com, last updated May 27, 2025, https://www.history.com/this-day-in-history/january-4/l-b-j-envisions-a-great-society-in-his-state-of-the-union-address.

Questions about the competence of elite leadership began creeping into public debate. Soon, riots in cities from Detroit to Asbury Park felt almost routine.

Meanwhile, the United States escalated in Vietnam. Bombing began in February, followed quickly by ground troops. Antiwar protests erupted on college campuses even as most Americans still supported the war. A surprising crack in elite control of the narrative appeared on AM radio, where rock and folk singers found a vast youth audience for protest songs.

As the year wore on, the antiwar movement grew—and authorities responded harshly. At a teach-in, professor Jim Mellen declared he would welcome a Viet Cong victory; he promptly lost his job at Drew University.[216] When burning draft cards spread as a protest tactic, Congress rushed through a law banning it. Johnson signed the measure, and three years later the Supreme Court upheld it, ruling it was not a violation of free speech.[217]

The draft itself was already unpopular, but its structure made it worse. College students were exempt. Staying in school meant staying out of Vietnam. Even with rising college enrollment, this policy tilted heavily toward affluent families. The gap between elites and everyone else widened further.

By the late 1960s, the nation seemed to be coming apart at the seams. Each summer brought riots, protests, and burning cities. In 1968, violence claimed the lives of Martin Luther King Jr. and Robert F. Kennedy. "The story of America's cultural revolution begins in 1968," observes the Manhattan Institute's Chris Rufo, who argues that the "long season of student uprisings, urban riots, and

---

216 Alex Williams, "Jim Mellen, an Original Member of the Militant Weathermen, Dies at 87," *The New York Times*, March 17, 2023, https://www.nytimes.com/2023/03/17/us/jim-mellen-dead.html.

217 United States v. O'Brien, 391 US 367 (1968).

revolutionary violence...provided the template for everything that followed."[218]

In 1969, the fired Drew University professor helped draft a manifesto for a militant group soon known as the Weathermen, later the Weather Underground. It called for "the destruction of US imperialism and the achievement of a classless world: world communism."[219]

In 1970, National Guardsmen killed four students protesting the Vietnam War at Kent State. Two years later, the Weather Underground and its allies were responsible for 1,900 domestic bombings—nearly five a day.[220] The pace made new attacks feel almost routine. At one point during my own high-school years, bomb threats became so common we were evacuated from school nearly every day.

This violence was driven by a radical ideology that explicitly rejected America's founding ideals. The Weathermen's manifesto declared that every American must choose: Either stand with "the United States as an oppressor nation" or with "the masses of people throughout the world whom U.S. imperialism is oppressing."[221]

Unsurprisingly, these ideas were deeply unpopular with voters. Yet they found traction among segments of the elite—particularly in academia. In response to the upheavals of the 1960s, the public went one way and academic elites went another. Authors of that manifesto—and even participants in the bombings—were later welcomed into college faculties.

---

218 Christopher F. Rufo, *America's Cultural Revolution* (Broadside Books: 2023) p. 2.

219 Williams, "Mellen."

220 Bryan Burrough, *Days of Rage* (Penguin Books: 2015), 2.

221 Karin Asbley et al., "You Don't Need a Weatherman To Know Which Way The Wind Blows," in *New Left Notes*, June 18, 1969, https://archive.org/stream/YouDontNeedAWeathermanToKnowWhichWayTheWindBlows_925/weather_djvu.txt.

Advocates of this radical creed became known as the New Left. On the surface, they shared certain concerns with traditional liberals, but they rejected the incremental reforms liberals pursued.

Traditional liberalism, notes Johns Hopkins professor Yascha Mounk, had "historically been characterized by its universalist aspirations. To be on the left was to insist that human beings are not defined by their religion or their skin color, by their upbringing or their sexual orientation." As Mounk explained, "A key goal of politics was to create a world in which we collectively realize that the things we share across identity lines are more important than the things that divide us."[222]

Those views echoed the immortal words of Thomas Jefferson—that all are created equal. Before the 1960s, most liberals shared that vision. Leaders like Frederick Douglass and Martin Luther King Jr. recognized that America had fallen short, but they remained optimistic about both the history and the promise of progress. Traditional liberals sought to extend the nation's founding ideals to all Americans. That was Dr. King's noble dream.

Traditional liberals, in short, defended traditional American values.

The New Left saw things very differently. They did not want reform; they wanted revolution.

In their view, writes Mounk, "trying to make progress toward a more just society by redoubling efforts to live up to such ideals…is a fool's errand."[223] They rejected the idea that progress had been—or could be—made. To them, America had always been, and would always remain, irredeemably racist: an oppressor nation, nothing more and nothing less.

Instead of striving for equality, the New Left demanded "public policies that explicitly make how someone is treated depend

---

[222] Yascha Mounk, *The Identity Trap* (Penguin Books: 2025), 8.

[223] Ibid., 11.

on the group to which they belong."[224] They also "reject universal values and neutral rules like free speech and equal opportunity as mere distractions that aim to…perpetuate the marginalization of minority groups."[225]

Few ideas could be more un-American than rejecting individual rights, free speech, and equality of opportunity. Yet that was the agenda the New Left sought to impose.

According to Rufo, "The activists of the radical Left want to replace individual rights with group-identity-based rights, enact a scheme of race-based wealth redistribution, and suppress speech based on a new racial and political calculus."[226] In today's terms, the views of the New Left would be associated with progressive—or "woke"—leaders.

The divide between traditional liberals and the New Left carries enormous consequences for American society. Traditional liberals and conservatives can argue fiercely about how best to live up to the nation's founding ideals of freedom, equality, and self-governance. But because they share those ultimate goals, they can still find common ground.

The New Left, by contrast, rejects those ideals altogether. Its "woke" or progressive ideology cannot engage in civil debate with either traditional liberals or conservatives.

To the New Left, anyone defending America's founding ideals is complicit in oppression. Defend free speech, and you are accused of trying to silence minorities. Call for a color-blind society, and you are branded an ally of White supremacists.

It is worth remembering that the intellectual foundations of this movement were laid by the same radicals who carried out thousands of domestic bombings in the early 1970s. A 1974 Weather

---

[224] Ibid., 64.

[225] Ibid., 11.

[226] Christopher F. Rufo, *America's Cultural Revolution* (Broadside Books: 2023), 5.

Underground manifesto rewrote history to declare that "the United States was founded on racism, sexism, slavery, and genocide."[227] The only solution, they insisted, was to tear everything down and let elite leaders rebuild from the rubble.

Debate was never the point. Knowing that most Americans rejected their views, New Left activists sought to silence dissent instead.

These ideas were radical then—and remain radical now. Yet as Chris Rufo has observed, "intellectuals of the New Left…silently rooted them into the entire range of America's knowledge-making institutions."[228] The result is that "the American university is now a 'counterinstitution,' driven by the ideology of the New Left."[229]

All this resulted from a perfect storm. The American university became embedded in middle-class life just as the nation underwent a cultural revolution. Academia adopted values the American people never embraced. Yet with the backing of *Wilsonian Government* and a centralized media, those New Left ideas were imposed on an unwilling nation.

Now, as American society decentralizes and new voices rise, that ideology is being pushed toward history's dustbin. The road to get there, however, will be turbulent.

---

[227] Ibid., 3.

[228] Ibid.

[229] Ibid., 43.

Chapter 10

IS SELF-GOVERNANCE EVEN POSSIBLE?

In the twenty-first century, America's founding ideals of freedom, equality, and self-governance are under sustained assault from two distinct but related strands of elitism: the Wilsonian model of government by unelected experts and the ideology of the New Left. Later chapters will explore how these rival worldviews clash and overlap. For now, the essential point is that both share a common premise: Ordinary Americans cannot be trusted to govern themselves. Elites—whether Progressive-era technocrats or twenty-first-century activists—assume the public is too ignorant, irrational, or apathetic to be taken seriously.

I strongly reject that assessment. Yet it is undeniable that most people are not deeply engaged in the nation's political dialogue. This raises a fair question: If citizens are inattentive, is self-governance even possible?

For more than two millennia before America's founding, political philosophers such as Socrates, Plato, and Aristotle insisted the answer was no. Is it possible they were right?

Modern scholars have echoed those doubts. Bernard Berelson described the "paradox of democracy": Citizens, in theory, are supposed to meet demanding standards of political knowledge—but in practice, most do not.[230] Others marvel that the United States has endured as a stable democracy despite evidence of an uninformed electorate.[231]

Walter Lippmann—a disciple of Woodrow Wilson and one of the most influential progressive journalists of the twentieth century—was especially blunt about the supposed failure of the American public. Democratic theory, he argued, requires citizens "to know what is going on and to have an opinion worth expressing on every question which confronts a self-governing community."[232] The impossibility of that standard was obvious even to Lippmann, who admitted that not even professional journalists like himself, let alone presidents, could achieve it.[233]

Since no one could measure up to Lippmann's theory of how democracy should work, he concluded democracy couldn't work. Like his mentor, President Wilson, Lippmann therefore decided that only unelected experts could be trusted to govern the country.

Later scholars went further. In *The Irony of Democracy,* Louis Schubert, Thomas R. Dye, and Harmon Zeigler dismissed self-governance outright, declaring that Lincoln's "government of the people, by the people, and for the people" had "no real-world meaning."[234]

If the skeptics are right, then everything I have argued in this book is wrong. More than that, everything the two Midwestern women—and millions of other Americans—were taught to believe about their country is wrong. Perhaps America is not exceptional after all. That is precisely what Schubert, Dye, and Zeigler suggest.

---

[230] Bernard R. Berelson et al., *Voting: A Study of Opinion Formation in a Presidential Campaign* (University of Chicago Press: 1986).

[231] Michael X. Delli Carpini and Scott Keeter, *What Americans Know about Politics and Why It Matters* (Yale University Press: 1997).

[232] Walter Lippman, *The Phantom Public* (Routledge: 1993), 4.

[233] Ibid.

[234] Thomas Dye et al., *The Irony of Democracy* 16th ed. (Wadsworth Publishing: 2013).

In their view, elites "govern all societies—democracies and dictatorships, capitalist and socialist, monarchies and theocracies, developing and industrialized."[235] In other words, the form of government does not matter.

Such views echo those of John Kenneth Galbraith, who, as noted earlier, claimed there was little difference between the US and Soviet economies because both were managed by bureaucratic elites. Galbraith, like Dye and his colleagues, failed to recognize the realities—and the benefits—of a self-governing society.

Schubert, Dye, and Zeigler went further, arguing that "life in U.S. democracy…is shaped by a tiny fraction of the population."[236] According to Dye, about 4,000 people determine the course of the nation, half of them graduates of just twelve elite universities.[237] Whether or not that figure is precise, the broader point is clear: Those wielding political influence represent only a minuscule share of the population.

Even if we count all 519,000 elected officials in America—from school board members to governors—they still comprise less than two-tenths of one percent of the nation. As political scientists Harold Lasswell and Daniel Lesser once observed, "Government is always government by the few, whether in the name of the few, the one, or the many."[238]

It is also true that voters often seem inattentive to matters political insiders deem important. Critics love to point out that most Americans cannot name their congressional representative. That charge is accurate. Yet why should voters bother? Roughly 90 percent live in districts where their "choice" has been nullified. Through gerrymandering, leaders of both parties have engineered a system that

[235] Ibid., 2.

[236] Ibid., 1.

[237] Dye, *Who's Running America?, p. 180*

[238] How . Dye, *Who's Running America?, p.3*

makes incumbents nearly untouchable. According to Ballotpedia, across four decades of competitive elections, incumbents have won an astonishing 94 percent of the time.[239]

Recent redistricting battles illustrate the problem vividly. Republican leaders in Texas redrew congressional maps to gain more GOP seats. In response, Governor Gavin Newsom and California Democrats sought to reshape their own maps to lock in Democratic advantages. Other states quickly followed suit. Both sides claimed they were merely responding to the unfair practices of the other team.

The spectacle resembled preschoolers shouting, "*They* started it!" Voters see through the charade: 74 percent recognize that both parties bend the rules when it benefits them.[240] The 10 percent of activists on the right cheer Republican maps, and the 10 percent on the left cheer Democratic ones. But for the vast majority, the maneuvering confirms a deeper truth: congressional "representation" is determined less by voters than by those who draw the lines.

Even when citizens do know their member of Congress, they also know that member is unlikely to listen. For most, the name hardly matters. If they need constituent services, they can Google it—a small act of self-service in a system that has forgotten self-governance.

In one sense, I welcome this. People should not be consumed by political trivia. It is good that Americans focus on raising families, doing their jobs, and building stronger communities. Those things matter far more than memorizing the roster of Washington players.

What is more troubling is how little the political class knows about the people it presumes to govern. Research by Johns Hopkins professors Jennifer Bachner and Benjamin Ginsberg shows that "official Washington seems to have an inaccurate view of popular

---

[239] "United States Congress Elections, 2024," Ballotpedia, accessed December 12, 2025, https://ballotpedia.org/United_States_Congress_elections,_2024#Incumbents_defeated_2.

[240] August 13–14, 2025—Napolitan News survey of 1,000 registered voters.

preferences."[241] My own surveys confirm the same point. Unlike the harmless gaps in public knowledge, elite ignorance about everyday America has serious consequences.

This brings us back to the central question: Is self-governance possible? I am confident it is. The reason is simple: those few who run government do not ultimately define the nation. They may control official policy, but genuine self-governance happens well beyond the formal structures of Washington.

At the dawn of the nineteenth century, Thomas Jefferson became America's third president. He envisioned the nation as an agrarian republic, trading with Europe for manufactured goods. Industry, in his view, was best left abroad.

But a young immigrant named Sam Slater had other plans. Having memorized the designs of British textile mills, he arrived in America the year George Washington took office and built the first US factory in Providence, Rhode Island. During Jefferson's presidency, Slater's system took root, and he became known as the "Father of the American Industrial Revolution."[242]

Slater's factories transformed American life. As Holy Cross professor Edward T. O'Donnell notes, they "changed the role of women in society, separating the spheres of home and work for the first time. Public education was born out of the factory town and the need for trained labor. Industrialized printing of everything from books to sheet music changed the face of entertainment.... We can even say that the Industrial Revolution led to the invention of time, at least our disciplined sense of it."[243]

The contrast was striking. Jefferson clung to an agrarian past, even commissioning a grand clock at Monticello that lacked a minute

---

[241] Bachner, Ginsberg were cited earlier, P 99.

[242] Edward T. O'Donnell, *Turning Points in American History, Lecture 11, The Great Courses, July 8, 2013.*

[243] Ibid.

hand—precision being unnecessary in a farm economy. Slater, by contrast, built the world Jefferson resisted. His factories introduced the rhythms of industrial time, reshaped communities, and propelled America into modernity.

Jefferson ran the government, but Slater helped shape the nation.

The so-called "paradox" of democracy dissolves once we distinguish between self-government and self-governance.

Self-government assumes that everything revolves around politics and formal institutions. It imagines that presidents, senators, kings, or bureaucrats determine both the fate of nations and the daily lives of citizens.

That assumption is false. Did Americans stop drinking alcohol during Prohibition? Was marijuana absent from the 1960s?

Self-governance recognizes that formal government is only one of many institutions shaping society. It has a role to play, but not the lead role. As Harvard historians Oscar and Mary Handlin observed, "Secure in the knowledge that the role of the government did not encompass every aspect of life, Americans created an apparatus of free institutions with which each group of them could seek its own goals without coercion."[244]

A self-governing society, rooted in freedom and respect for individuals, empowers each American to pursue dreams of their own choosing. That's the kind of society that lets someone like Ted Benna to pioneer 401(k) plans and revolutionize retirement savings. He didn't have to be a government official. The result is a stronger, more prosperous nation.

This dynamic remains visible today. In the 2008 presidential election, Senator John McCain's rallying cry was "Drill, baby, drill." His opponent, Barack Obama, countered, "We can't just drill our

[244] Oscar and Mary Handlin, *The Dimensions of Liberty* (Harvard University Press: 1961), 5.

way out of this problem."[245] Yet while Obama was in office, the United States became the world's largest producer of crude oil.[246]

This did not happen because Obama changed course. As president, he sought to restrain crude oil production. But demand for energy could not be wished away, and innovation was not under Washington's control. Private-sector advances in hydraulic fracturing reshaped global energy markets, reduced America's dependence on foreign oil, and lowered prices for working families.

Consider the broader pattern: Nearly every transformative change of the twenty-first century has come from outside Washington. Has anything altered daily life more than the smartphone? Will anything transform society more in the decade ahead than artificial intelligence?

Schubert, Dye, and Zeigler—professors convinced that elites control government, which in turn controls society—defined power as "deciding who gets what, when, and how."[247] That description applies less to Washington than to Amazon. In the twenty-first century, Google, Facebook, Tesla, Airbnb, Uber, Instagram, Netflix, and countless other innovators have shaped daily life far more than the federal government ever could.

These companies thrived by responding to the choices of individual Americans. That is the opposite of politics, where leaders demand that voters focus on whatever official Washington deems important. Google makes it easy to find information you want; government agencies make it hard.

---

[245] Nicholas Loris, "Obama Was Wrong on Oil. We Did 'Drill Our Way Out of the Problem,'" The Heritage Foundation, September 14, 2018, https://www.heritage.org/energy-economics/commentary/obama-was-wrong-oil-we-did-drill-our-way-out-the-problem.

[246] Ibid.

[247] Dye, *The Irony*.

The greater the sphere of individual freedom, the more likely positive change emerges outside government. Perhaps that is why so many elitists insist Americans already enjoy too much freedom.

One overlooked form of freedom is the ability to "vote with your feet." When the pandemic struck, my wife and I were living in Manhattan. One evening, while dining outdoors, we talked about moving to Florida. A woman at the next table—a complete stranger—suddenly shouted: "You can't move to Florida until they get a new governor—DeSantis will kill you!"

Her outburst underscored a vital truth. She was free to stay in New York, where she believed policies were safer. We were free to leave, as thousands of others did. That simple freedom—both her freedom to stay and our freedom to walk away—constrains local governments more than the ballot box ever could.

Typical turnout in mayoral elections is only about 20 percent, according to University of Chicago professor Christopher Barry, who calls the figure "shockingly low."[248] School board and other local elections draw even fewer voters, sometimes just 5 to 8 percent.

One humorous example of low-turnout democracy comes from Collin County, Texas. Founded in 1846 with Buckner as its county seat, the county soon held an election to consider moving the seat to McKinney. Election Day was marred by inclement weather, and only eleven people voted. McKinney won and remains the county seat today.

Despite that miniscule turnout, a more recent case on Long Island was even more absurd. Brookhaven held a referendum where

---

[248] Christopher R. Berry, "The Timing of Local Elections," The University of Chicago Center for Effective Government, Democracy Reform Primer Series, January 25, 2024, https://effectivegov.uchicago.edu/primers/the-timing-of-local-elections.

no one voted. Not a single person—not even a town employee or a resident with something to gain—showed up.[249]

When turnout hovers at a dozen ballots (or even at 5 to 20 percent), you cannot claim the result reflects public sentiment. Such anemic participation also gives partisan activists room to game the process.

Yet even when local elections draw meager turnout, communities remain accountable. The real force is not voting but the ability of residents to walk away. In the 1950s, Northwestern University professor Charles Tiebout noted that cities and towns compete vigorously for people, jobs, businesses, and revenue.[250]

I once lived in a small town that hosted festivals nearly every month—Christmas, Halloween, the Fourth of July, wine tastings, concerts. The events were fun but also brought traffic and parking headaches. Was it worth it? Different people answered differently. That is the essence of a self-governing society: Individuals can decide for themselves. The mayor and council set policy, but residents choose how to respond.

Tiebout likened citizens to customers, weighing costs (taxes, commute times, other inconveniences) against benefits such as schools, parks, shopping, transit, and cultural amenities. In that light, local mayors resemble chief marketing officers more than rulers. Their job is to offer the right mix to keep current residents and attract new ones.

And if citizens dislike the package, they need not campaign for a new mayor or lobby city hall—they can leave. Political scientist Albert Hirschman called this the power of "exit." Too many exits are a warning sign: Governments must adjust or decline. As Hirschman

---

[249] Zach Williams, "Long Island officials stunned after no one votes in referendum," *New York Post*, August 15, 2022, https://nypost.com/2022/08/15/brookhaven-long-island-officials-stunned-after-no-one-votes-in-referendum/.

[250] Charles M. Tiebout, "A Pure Theory of Local Expenditures," in *The Journal of Political Economy* 64, no. 5 (October 1956), 416–424.

put it, "[E]xit has an essential role to play in restoring quality performance of government, just as in any organization."[251]

In short, governments can set policies, but people decide for themselves whether to stay—and whether those policies make sense.

The power to walk away also reshapes politics at the state level. In recent years, residents have been leaving New York, New Jersey, Illinois, and California for Florida, Texas, and the Carolinas. Businesses are leaving as well. There are now more bank and finance industry jobs in Texas than in New York.[252] *Bloomberg* reports that both California and New York have lost firms managing a trillion dollars in financial assets.[253]

Each departure sends a warning signal to the governments they leave behind.

Of course, exit is not easy. People wrestle with whether to stay and try to improve their community or move on. For some—especially those who can work remotely—the decision is simpler than for others whose livelihoods are tied to a specific place. Precisely because it is difficult, exit carries force.

There is also another side to the equation. Sometimes moves are driven by jobs, schools, or family circumstances beyond anyone's control. In those cases, the real power lies in deciding where to go. Americans are free to choose states and communities that best match their preferred mix of costs and benefits.

---

[251] Hirschman, *Exit,* 117.

[252] Carl Campanile, "JPMorgan Chase now employs more workers in Texas than NY—top city biz advocate calls it 'scary' development," *New York Post*, September 29, 2025, https://nypost.com/2025/09/29/us-news/jpmorgan-chase-now-employs-more-workers-in-texas-than-ny-top-city-biz-advocate-calls-it-scary-development/.

[253] Linly Lin and Tom Maloney, "New York and California Each Lost $1 Trillion When Financial Firms Moved South," *Bloomberg*, August 21, 2023, https://www.bloomberg.com/graphics/2023-asset-management-relocation-wall-street-south/?srnd=premium&sref=MTy2GeXk.

It's important to recognize that people voting with their feet also benefits those who remain behind. Political leaders are severely constrained by the need to keep a community attractive for new potential residents. That practical limitation is the best protection a community can have from its politicians.

How much does this ability to "exit" limit government power? One clue lies in how much political leaders despise it. As Albert Hirschman observed, in politics the power to leave has often been branded "criminal," condemned as desertion, defection, or even treason.[254] Elites want citizens trapped in their games of voice and loyalty. But exit forces governments to respond to real-world incentives.

Hirschman also reminded us that America itself was built on exit. "The United States owes its very existence and growth to millions of decisions choosing exit over voice."[255] The Pilgrims had no power to reform the king's established church, so they left to worship in freedom.

Exit is vital, but it is only one tool of self-governance. Another is the freedom to associate with others of our own choosing.

To modern Americans, forming clubs, charities, businesses, and political groups without government permission seems normal. For most of human history, it was radical. In colonial America, it was revolutionary. When religious refugees settled in Massachusetts, they quickly saw the need for higher education and resolved to start a college. Yet as subjects of the British Crown, they faced a problem: Under English law, no association or institution could be formed without the king's approval.

The colonists recognized that the king might have granted permission to establish a college—but he would have done so only on his terms. It would have been rooted in Anglican theology, the very creed the colonists had crossed the Atlantic to escape. At best, they

---

[254] Hirschman, *Exit*, 17.

[255] Hirschman, *Exit*, 106.

might have begged for a token course or two on alternative views. But the entrepreneurial colonists had something else in mind.

So, in 1636 they simply founded a college without asking permission. That college was Harvard. Its creation was illegal, but the king was too distant—and too distracted by the coming English Civil War—to intervene. Eventually the king lost his head, but Harvard endured. Yale and other institutions soon followed, also founded without royal sanction.

The consequences were profound. By the time of the American Revolution, seven of the nine colonial colleges were technically illegal. Yet they became hubs of leadership in the struggle for independence.

More importantly, the precedent of unauthorized association spread rapidly. In the 140 years between Harvard's founding and the Declaration of Independence, colonists formed countless organizations to combat poverty, expand education, fight for abolition, publish newspapers, and launch businesses. Under British law, these associations were unlawful. In America, they became the backbone of a free and self-governing society.

Like exit, freedom of association has long been despised by those in power. In the 1950s, Alabama accused the NAACP of aiding the Montgomery Bus Boycott without state approval. Officials demanded the names and addresses of all members and agents—a transparent attempt to harass and intimidate supporters.

The dispute reached the Supreme Court. In 1958, the Court unanimously sided with the NAACP. Writing for the Court, Justice John Marshall Harlan II affirmed that "freedom to engage in association…is an inseparable aspect of the 'liberty' assured by the Due Process Clause of the Fourteenth Amendment."[256]

---

[256] David L. Hudson Jr., "Freedom of Association," Free Speech Center, last updated May 5, 2025, https://firstamendment.mtsu.edu/article/freedom-of-association/.

So what does all this mean for the question of whether self-governance is possible?

These examples show that governing is about far more than formal institutions. Through the power to walk away and the freedom to associate without permission, ordinary Americans have repeatedly reshaped the nation.

In practice, self-governance is not only possible; it is the only way society can function. Every choice we make about whom to associate with is also a choice about how we will be governed. Marriage, employment, church membership, joining a theater troupe—each comes with obligations freely accepted. In making those commitments, we decide who will help govern our lives.

Everyone has a role in a self-governing society. And everyone has a choice about the communities and institutions they will live under.

Government is just one institution among many. It plays a role, but not the lead role. Most citizens rightly devote most of their attention to raising families, pursuing careers, and building communities. They delegate much of the political work to elected officials, but they always retain the right to decide how to respond.

In this situation, voters know many things that are vital to their daily lives even if they are not aware of political trivia. And there are many things that politicians don't know that actually hold our society together and make everything work. That is why what America's politicians don't know about America is far more dangerous than what Americans don't know about politics.

Chapter 11

WHERE DO WE GO FROM HERE?

To win the battle for America's soul—and to pass on a bright future to our children and grandchildren—the most important thing we can do is restore a self-governing society. That is what made the United States an exceptional nation, and it remains the best hope we can offer future generations.

The question, then, is how to do that in a time of toxic polarization. How do we repair a broken political system when two lifelong Midwestern friends—women who share values, history, and community—now feel trapped on opposite sides of a battlefield?

It's important to recognize that while the 80 percent choose one team or the other on Election Day, the choice often says more about the media and social ecosystems they inhabit than their political views and hopes for the nation. They aren't counting on much from their political team but are repeatedly told the other team is worse. It's a bit like going to a Super Bowl party when your own team isn't playing. To be social, you pick a side to root for, but you're not all that engaged.

To such casual observers, the volume of unpleasant political noise makes it sound as though both sides are equally to blame. However, that perception misses an important truth.

Since the 1960s, the cultural and political "progressive vanguard" has been the driving force behind efforts to undermine America's founding ideals and remake its culture. As Justin Vassallo described it in *The Liberal Patriot*, these elitists favor "mass migration, trans activism for kids, and inculcating schools and businesses with 'anti-racist' and 'decolonial' practices."[257]

Conservatives and populists, including Donald Trump, have been largely reacting to that agenda. Their response has often been messy and angry, but it starts from a desire to defend what the Left seeks to overturn. That is one reason so many people can approve of Trump's policies without liking the way he gets things done.

In our 10/10/80 nation, the warring ten-percenters insist that America's survival hinges on the next election. They are wrong, but they are loud—very loud. Each side claims to be the only force capable of protecting the country from the supposed dangers of the other. Some dream of crushing their opponents in a final battle for control of Congress and the White House. Others want to tear the system apart and rebuild it in their own image. Still others harbor a deep resentment toward the elites and want to see the powerful stripped of their influence.

Because they are true believers, the ten-percenters keep yelling at the 80 percent and insisting that the most important thing anyone can do is vote. They urge people to set aside everything else and vote for the right team. The emphasis on voting resonates with the two Midwestern women—and with many others. It's what they were brought up to believe in.

Voting is important, but it is far from the only responsibility of citizens in a self-governing society.

---

[257] Justin Vassallo, "Democrats Are Losing the Culture War," The Liberal Patriot, October 13, 2025, https://www.liberalpatriot.com/p/democrats-are-losing-the-culture.

That doesn't mean national politics should be ignored. Congressional elections still matter—a great deal. Who controls the House and Senate after the 2026 midterms will determine whether Washington spends two years chasing impeachment or challenging the New Left's ideological dominance. But self-governance cannot be outsourced to Washington. Voting is the starting point of citizenship, not the finish line. The harder work begins at home—in our families, communities, and local institutions.

More to the point, voters do not have the power to "throw the bums out." In the 2026 midterms, only about 5 to 10 percent of Americans will live in districts where they have a real choice about who represents them.[258] The other 90 to 95 percent are trapped in districts engineered to ensure that only one candidate has any chance of winning. That is why, for four decades, congressional incumbents have been reelected 94 percent of the time.[259]

The hard truth is that members of Congress are not chosen by voters at all. They are chosen by the politicians and party operatives who draw the maps. Call it what you want—but it is not representative democracy.

The elitist scholars who wrote *The Irony of Democracy* went so far as to claim that elections have "only symbolic value." In their view, the purpose of voting is merely to keep the masses tied to the system by giving them something to do on Election Day.[260] Sadly, there is more truth to that today than either political team wants to admit.

But, that's not how it's supposed to be in our country. To most Americans, this feels like a genuine crisis of democracy. For the 80 percent not consumed by partisan warfare—including the two Midwestern women—the instinctive response is to fix the system:

---

258 "2026 CPR House Race Ratings," *The Cook Political Report*, December 9, 2025, https://www.cookpolitical.com/ratings/house-race-ratings.

259 "United States Congress Elections, 2024."

260 Dye, *The Irony*, 5.

to reform elections so voters are in charge and politicians are held accountable.

That instinct is understandable, but it is not realistic in today's environment. One of my most important jobs as a pollster is to tell people what they need to hear, not what they want to hear. And what those who care about restoring self-governance need to hear is that fixing Congress directly is not a top priority right now. We should absolutely vote, express our views on important issues, and get involved in campaigns.

However, we should not invest our energy in trying to fix Congress itself.

Why? Because Americans today lack the power to fix Congress at the ballot box—or anywhere else—through direct means. As frustrating as that sounds, it is a reality check that calls for a change of perspective. Think of the story I shared earlier about sorting yams after church. When my family focused on the remaining pile, we were demoralized. Everything changed when we looked at what had already been accomplished.

In the same way, those committed to renewing self-governance must stop looking to Washington as the arena of reform. The more productive path is to bring about change closer to home, using every tool at our disposal instead of getting lost in the partisan games of Congress. That often means relying on state and local officials to take power back from the federal government—one step at a time.

For those still skeptical, consider this: Under current law, each representative in Congress supposedly represents roughly 750,000 people. Even the most diligent and attentive member cannot meaningfully reflect the views of so many constituents. In practice, most "representatives" know their districts only as demographic cross-tabs in a poll.

Over time, I concluded that the only way to make Congress more responsive would be to create much smaller districts. This was not a novel idea. George Washington and James Madison both believed representatives should be closely tied to the people. Washington argued that no member of Congress should represent more than 30,000 citizens.[261] In today's world, I would be satisfied with one representative for every 100,000.

Smaller districts would almost certainly improve accountability. My own experience with the term-limits movement showed that the smaller the district, the more responsive legislators became. Twenty-two states allowed voters to place initiatives on the ballot, and in every single one, voters approved term limits. Yet state legislatures—protective of their own power—refused to impose limits on their congressional delegations. We came close in North Carolina, but only New Hampshire's legislature followed through.

Why New Hampshire? Because it has the smallest legislative districts in the nation. Each state representative serves fewer than 3,500 people, and state senators fewer than 60,000. That scale forces elected officials to stay close to the public and far from the political bubble.

By contrast, California has the largest state legislative districts in America. Each state senator represents about a million people. When voters imposed term limits there in 1990, lawmakers reacted with fury and have spent decades trying to chip away at the voter-imposed restrictions.

Even though I am convinced that smaller districts would improve Congress, I no longer spend time pursuing that reform. Why? Because there is no way voters can do anything about it under current conditions. Only Congress has the constitutional authority to increase its own membership, and members have no incentive to dilute their power. The odds that Congress itself will create smaller districts are about as slim as the odds they will impose term limits on themselves. It's simply not going to happen under any circumstances.

---

[261] Bruce Bartlett, *Enlarging the House of Representatives,* New York Times, January 7, 2014

Any strategy to restore a self-governing society—or to achieve any political goal—must have at least a reasonable chance of success. Otherwise, it risks turning frustration into despair. We live in a nation where many are angry at government's failures and unresponsiveness. Convincing seethingly angry voters to chase strategies with no chance of success is not only wasteful; it is dangerous.

This is precisely the trap set by many of the ten-percenters and self-serving political leaders. They rile up supporters with crusades that cannot succeed but are useful for fundraising and virtue-signaling. Political scientist Aaron Wildavsky, writing more than half a century ago, warned that this dynamic was "a recipe for violence." To win elections, politicians "promise a lot; deliver a little."[262] They encourage people to believe things will dramatically improve, only to disappoint them once in office. The inevitable result is even deeper anger.

Wildavsky's warning came in 1968, a year seared into American memory. President John F. Kennedy had been assassinated just five years earlier. In 1968, both Martin Luther King Jr. and Robert Kennedy were gunned down. Riots raged in more than a hundred cities. Anti-war protests and civil-rights demonstrations shook the nation, culminating in violence outside the Democratic National Convention in Chicago.

Sadly, Wildavsky's words resonate just as powerfully in twenty-first-century America. The assassination of Charlie Kirk shocked the nation, as did two separate attempts on Donald Trump's life. In 2025, two Minnesota legislators were murdered, and the year before, Pennsylvania Governor Josh Shapiro was forced to flee when his residence was set on fire. Even the private sector has not been immune: When Elon Musk was directing the DOGE effort, Tesla cars and dealerships were torched in coordinated attacks.

---

[262] Wildavsky, *Revolt Against the Masses*

This eruption of anger helps explain Donald Trump's disruptive rise. Unlike the ten-percenters who shout without effect, he actually rattled the Capitol. In *The Hunger Games* metaphor I used earlier, he became a kind of president of District 13—fighting the New Left with the very tools of Wilsonian Government.

His approach shook the system, but disruption alone is not the same as renewal. Breaking the Capitol's hold was necessary, yet it did not by itself restore a self-governing society. For those committed to restoring America's founding ideals of freedom, equality, and self-governance, the challenge is to channel the energy of the seethingly angry in a constructive direction.

The best example of how to do that comes from the Rev. Dr. Martin Luther King Jr.'s leadership during the Montgomery Bus Boycott. At that time, Black voters in the South had virtually no voice in politics. To many White leaders, this meant they could be ignored with impunity.

The injustices fueling Black anger in the 1950s were far greater than anything most Americans face today. Supreme Court Justice Clarence Thomas, who grew up in a Georgia home without running water under Jim Crow, once reflected on this. At a gathering where someone lamented how much freedom has supposedly been lost in modern America, Thomas reportedly replied: "That's not how it feels to me."

Thomas grew up in a world where freedom didn't exist for most Black Americans. He was seven when Rosa Parks's refusal to surrender her seat on a Montgomery bus highlighted very real daily indignities. Three-quarters of bus riders were Black, yet the company refused to hire Black drivers.[263] Riders were forced to sit in the back, surrender seats to Whites, and endure routine disrespect. Still,

[263] Martin Luther King Jr., *Stride Toward Freedom: The Montgomery Story* (Harpercollins Childrens Books: 1987), p. 37.

approximately 17,500 Black riders relied on the buses twice a day to reach their jobs.[264]

Boycotting the system demanded extraordinary sacrifice. Organizing carpools, walking miles to work, and enduring harassment required commitment and hope that their efforts would build a better world. It was far more difficult than symbolic consumer protests today—like refusing to buy a Tesla because Elon Musk worked with Donald Trump. Success required perseverance rooted in vision and faith.

And just as important, King's movement offered a positive story that appealed far beyond his immediate followers. It drew in people who were not themselves the victims of Jim Crow but who could see injustice clearly once it was put before them. That is the lesson for our 10/10/80 nation today: The 80 percent in the middle are not truly enemies. They are neighbors who often live in different media and social worlds. The challenge is to help them look behind the curtain together, as King helped America see the moral reality of segregation.

That was where King's leadership made the difference. He aimed for a lasting victory, not the cheap theatrics of "owning" the other side or venting justified rage in public. He warned that undisciplined protest would "end up as a meaningless drama on the stage of history."[265]

At just twenty-six years old and new to Montgomery, King could easily have won applause from the angriest voices by railing against the bus company, the city council, or the White community. He could have urged vandalism or violent protest. Instead, he chose a higher goal: making Montgomery better.

King devoted himself to channeling the community's justified anger into disciplined, constructive action. He explained his strategy, asked for trust, and prepared people for how hard the journey would

---

[264] Ibid, p. 57.

[265] Ibid, p. 53

be. He reminded them to stay disciplined—even to turn the other cheek when provoked.

The obstacles were immense, and Montgomery's White leaders escalated at every step. The boycott's offices began in the Alabama Negro Baptist Center, but White churches funding the center pressured it to evict them. New offices had to be found.[266] Black taxi drivers tried to help by charging only ten cents—the same as bus fare—but the police commissioner shut them down by threatening to revoke their licenses unless they charged the legal minimum of forty-five cents.[267]

In response, King's team created what we would now call a ride-sharing service. Churches and individuals volunteered cars and time to shuttle Black workers to their jobs. It worked—until city leaders leaned on insurers to drop coverage for participating drivers. The city council then outlawed the system altogether and used the new law to justify mass arrests.[268]

Officials also adopted a "get tough" policy of enforcing even the smallest infractions. King himself was arrested—officially for driving thirty miles per hour in a twenty-five zone. He reframed it with characteristic clarity: He was arrested, he said, for "the crime of desiring for my people the unalienable rights of life, liberty, and the pursuit of happiness."[269]

One night, as King spoke at a mass meeting about the need to avoid violence, his home was bombed—with his wife and child inside. Thankfully, they survived. In a remarkable act of leadership, King told his followers: "If one day you find me sprawled out dead, I do not want you to retaliate with a single act of violence. I urge you

---

[266] Ibid, p. 66.
[267] Ibid, p. 60.
[268] Ibid, p. 119
[269] Ibid, p. 113.

to continue protesting with the same dignity and discipline you have shown so far."[270] That is leadership.

The intimidation did not stop there. King's request for a firearm permit was denied. The homes of other boycott leaders were bombed, along with their churches. Harassment, arrests, and violence continued for more than a year before the US Supreme Court finally ruled that bus segregation was unconstitutional.[271] Even then, violence against Montgomery's Black community persisted.

Through it all, King succeeded in channeling anger toward disciplined resistance. The community's strategic discipline exposed who was truly in the wrong. Even after homes and churches were bombed and people were shot, King and his followers refused to let rage become the story. Their perseverance showed, day after day, who the real enemy was.

And when the boycott ended in victory, King again displayed extraordinary leadership. Rather than claiming triumph over his opponents, he told his followers: "We must not take this as a victory over the white man, but as a victory for justice and democracy."[272]

That is the kind of leadership America needs today. It did not depend on getting people to the polls—King's followers were not even allowed to vote. It was leadership that recognized there is more to governing society than winning the next election or wielding government power against opponents.

It is a leadership that, in King's own words, "does not seek to defeat or humiliate the opponent, but to win his friendship and understanding."[273] It is a leadership that acknowledges our differences but also recognizes something more important that unites

[270] Ibid, p. 102.
[271] Ibid, p. 121.
[272] Ibid, p. 123.
[273] Ibid, p. 79.

us: We are all heirs to the same legacy—America's founding ideals of freedom, equality, and self-governance.

And ultimately, that kind of leadership proved capable of moving even Washington itself. It was a reminder that moral renewal at the local level is what gives Congress its conscience.

The ten-percenters on each side of the partisan divide would prefer endless political war, where the victors impose top-down solutions and everyone else is told that their only job is to vote.

To restore a self-governing society, we need a different approach—one that uses every tool at our disposal to bring about change in Washington. But to craft such a strategy, we must first see clearly the political moment we are living in today.

Despite the obstacles before us, I remain an optimist. America's best days are not behind us; they lie ahead. The American people still believe in our founding ideals, even when their leaders do not. That belief is the most powerful resource we have. It is what toppled segregation, what fueled the march for independence, and what will one day restore a truly self-governing society.

Chapter 12

SETTING THE STAGE

As the 1970s closed, the Great Turnaround had just gotten started. President Carter convened a commission of scholars, politicians, business leaders, union chiefs, and activists to draft a national agenda for the 1980s. The string of razor-thin elections that would one day culminate in Donald Trump's rise to the White House was still a decade away.

The commission members disagreed on many issues, but they shared a single anxiety: "The last decade has witnessed the beginnings of a trend away from centralized authority."[274] To them, that trend posed a grave danger. A nation that slipped the grip of centralized control, they feared, might become "ungovernable."[2] By ungovernable, of course, they meant a country where people like them no longer set the agenda. Their vision echoed John Kenneth Galbraith's worldview, where innovation flowed only from large organizations and central governments.

Predictably, the remedies they considered would further insulate Washington from voters. Some proposed electing members of Congress to four-year terms rather than two, so they would face the

[274] President's Commission, "A National Agenda for the Eighties," University of Michigan Library, January 1, 1980.

public half as often. Others suggested a single six-year presidential term, eliminating the possibility of reelection altogether.[275]

What the report never mentioned—astonishing in hindsight—was the one force that would ultimately undermine their authority: computers. The word never appeared, not in reference to the massive machines then housed in government and corporate basements, nor to the personal computers that were about to revolutionize daily life. Nor was there mention of satellites or the rise of cable television.

Like the Galactic Empire in *Star Wars*, America's political elites were prepared to defend their power against visible, large-scale threats. But they could not conceive of smaller, more agile forces dismantling their dominance. The notion that their hold on power could be shattered by the personal computer seemed as far-fetched as Luke Skywalker taking down the Death Star with a single, well-placed shot.

Steve Jobs and Bill Gates were not at the table because they were unknown at the time. Besides, they were too busy building technologies that would transform the world in ways the Carter commission could not fathom. Had they walked into the room to share their vision, the young entrepreneurs would likely have been laughed out of it.

In short, America's political and cultural elites had no idea what was unfolding around them. Digital entrepreneur Mitch Kapor later remarked: "Nobody in Washington, D.C., took [the Internet] seriously, so it was allowed to happen. By the time anybody noticed, it had already won."[276]

As American society was beginning to decentralize, political leaders marched in the opposite direction. They expanded bureaucracy

---

[275] Ibid.

[276] Nico Mele, End of Big, St. Martin's Press, p 23.

rather than adapting to the new reality. Today, the number of government regulators is five times higher than it was in the 1970s.[277]

Even as the Wilsonian model of centralized government grew larger, public trust collapsed. In the early 1960s, more than 70 percent of voters trusted the federal government to do the right thing most of the time. A decade later, that number fell below 50 percent.[278] By the early 1970s, distrust had become the majority view—a fragile foundation on which to build an ever-expanding bureaucracy. Elites failed to notice.

Voters did. They responded by electing Ronald Reagan, who famously quipped that the nine most terrifying words in the English language are: "I'm from the government, and I'm here to help."[279] Elites recoiled at that line. Voters embraced it. Reagan won forty-four states in his first election and forty-nine the second time. Over the course of two elections, therefore, Reagan carried ninety-three states and lost only seven.[280]

Remarkably, trust in government actually rose during his presidency. Think about that: the leader most skeptical of federal power managed to increase public confidence in it. For Wilsonian elitists—who saw experts and bureaucrats as the solution to every problem—this was a bitter irony. For voters, it affirmed their own instincts.

---

[277] Scott Rasmussen, Number of the Day, Ballotpedia, April 3, 2017 https://ballotpedia.org/Scott_Rasmussen%27s_Number_of_the_Day_for_April_3,_2017

[278] "Public Trust in Government: 1958–2025," Pew Research Center, December 4, 2025, https://www.pewresearch.org/politics/2025/12/04/public-trust-in-government-1958-2025/.

[279] Ronald Reagan, "The President's News Conference," archived by Ronald Reagan Presidential Library and Museum, August 12, 1986, https://www.reaganlibrary.gov/archives/speech/presidents-news-conference-23.

[280] Leip, *Election Atlas.*

Even today, sixty-two percent of Americans agree with Reagan's warning about government "help."[281]

Trust ticked upward again in the 1990s when Bill Clinton declared, "The era of big government is over."[282] Voters likely appreciated that the president at least acknowledged their skepticism. Working with House Speaker Newt Gingrich, Clinton even managed to briefly balance the federal budget.[283]

Still, those moments of renewed trust were fleeting. The long-term trend has moved steadily downward for decades. It has now been more than half a century since most Americans trusted their government most of the time.[284]

This erosion of confidence did not begin with Trump, Obama, or any other twenty-first-century president. It is not a sudden crisis unique to our time. The decline began more than sixty years ago, in the shadow of the Vietnam War, and it has continued ever since as government centralized while society itself grew more decentralized.

That decline also helps explain today's polarization. The anger broadcast on cable news creates the impression of a nation locked in permanent partisan war. In reality, most Americans—the eighty percent—are not hardened partisans. They are weary of the political game-playing on both sides. Yet as distrust deepened, and as Americans sorted into separate media and social ecosystems, even neighbors with shared concerns came to see one another as opponents.

All this leaves us in uncharted waters. Nearly sixty percent of Americans alive today were born after 1972—the last time government

[281] November 28–29, 2023—Napolitan News survey of 1,000 registered voters.

[282] Bill Clinton, 1996 State of the Union Address

[283] "Federal Surplus or Deficit," FRED, updated October 16, 2025, https://fred.stlouisfed.org/series/FYFSD.

[284] Pew Center Data cited earlier

was trusted by most voters.[285] In other words, most citizens have never known an era when trust in Washington was the norm.

Elites, however, remain oblivious. A recent survey of the Elite One Percent found that sixty-five percent believe most voters still trust government most of the time.[286] Sixty-one percent even claimed most voters believe their own member of Congress is the best person for the job.[287] They are wrong on both counts.

This disconnect—elites refusing to recognize reality—is one reason Reagan was the last president to win a true landslide. Before we explore how America moved from Reagan to Trump, it is worth pausing to recall the political landscape leading into the era of ten straight close elections.

Prior to 1988, Republicans had won four of the previous five presidential contests, three of them in landslides.[288] To many commentators of that time, it appeared as if the GOP had an unbreakable lock on the Electoral College.[289] Twenty-five states with 234 electoral votes had gone Republican in all five of those elections. Another ten states, totaling 117 electoral votes, had voted Republican in at least four of the five. With 270 votes needed to win, the GOP could plausibly claim a base of 351.[290]

By contrast, Democrats had little to celebrate. Only the District of Columbia, with its three electoral votes, backed their nominee in

---

285 "Census Bureau Releases New U.S. Population Estimates by Age and Sex," US Census Bureau, April 10, 2025, https://www.census.gov/newsroom/press-releases/2025/population-estimates-age-sex.html.

286 April 23–28, 2024—Napolitan Institute survey of 500 elites.

287 Ibid.

288 Leip, *Election Atlas*.

289 Steven Taylor, "Whatever Happened to the Republican 'Lock' on the Electoral College?" in *New England Journal of Political Science* 7, no. 1 (2013).

290 Leip, *Election Atlas*, calculated by author.

all five elections. Only one state—Minnesota, with ten votes—went Democratic in four of the five.[291]

There was little doubt by the late 1980s that Republican presidents had secured a governing mandate. The GOP candidate effectively began each race with a base of 351 Electoral College votes, while Democrats started with only thirteen. Given those numbers, it seemed the Democrats would need a miracle to win. Few imagined the country was on the brink of four decades of razor-thin elections.

In that environment, Vice President George H. W. Bush sought the top job. An honorable man, Bush had enlisted in the Navy as a teenager and earned medals for valor in World War II. At age twenty, he narrowly survived after his plane was shot down over the Pacific. After the war, he graduated from Yale and entered Congress in 1966. Over the next two decades, he served as ambassador to the UN, chairman of the Republican National Committee, US envoy to China, director of the CIA, and vice president.[292]

Bush's résumé—like Hillary Clinton's a generation later—made him a dream candidate for the political establishment. For many Reagan loyalists, however, those insider credentials bred suspicion. Making matters worse, Bush had called Reagan's tax-cutting plan "voodoo economics."[293]

Full disclosure: I was one of the skeptics. Knowing my state's vote was not in doubt, I wrote in another name on the 1988 ballot—an act that earned me a stern lecture from a poll worker about throwing my vote away.

---

[291] Ibid.

[292] "George H. W. Bush," The White House Historical Association, accessed December 12, 2025, https://www.whitehousehistory.org/bios/george-bush.

[293] Brian Domitrovic, "George H. W. Bush's Voodoo Rhetoric," *Forbes*, December 2, 2018, https://www.forbes.com/sites/briandomitrovic/2018/12/02/george-h-w-bushs-voodoo-rhetoric/.

To calm conservative concerns, Bush made one of the clearest campaign pledges in modern politics: "Read my lips: no new taxes."[294] The promise was pressed by speechwriter Peggy Noonan, though Bush's policy team resisted.[295] It worked. Riding Reagan's coattails, Bush won 53 percent of the popular vote and became the last candidate to surpass four hundred Electoral College votes.[296]

Even then, the Red Wall appeared intact. After Bush's victory, twenty-three states had voted Republican in six straight elections, and another eight had done so in five of six. No candidate since has topped Bush's share of the popular vote.[297]

Once in office, however, Bush broke his tax pledge. The *New York Post* headline was brutal: "Read My Lips: I Lied."[298] That breach shattered the Reagan coalition, deepened conservative distrust of establishment Republicans and helped launch the populist rebellion Trump would later lead.

The immediate consequence was Ross Perot's third-party run. The eccentric billionaire surged to the top of the polls in early 1992, dropped out mid-campaign, and reentered to capture 19 percent of the vote.[299] His insurgent bid gave Democrats the opening they needed. Bill Clinton won the presidency with just 43 percent of the popular vote.[300]

That same year, John DiStaso, a political reporter for the *New Hampshire Union Leader* popularized a new label—RINO, "Republican

---

[294] Ibid.

[295] Bob Woodward, "Origin of the Tax Pledge," *The Washington Post*, October 4, 1992, https://www.washingtonpost.com/archive/politics/1992/10/04/origin-of-the-tax-pledge/b669c4fc-79b2-4d2d-8289-c0398e3e2895/.

[296] Leip, *Election Atlas*.

[297] Ibid.

[298] Bill Schneider, "Dwell on jobs, not cuts," *Politico*, June 7, 2011, https://www.politico.com/story/2011/06/dwell-on-jobs-not-cuts-056344.

[299] Leip, *Election Atlas*.

[300] Ibid.

in Name Only."[301] Though Trump was not yet on the scene, the distrust that would fuel his movement had already become a defining feature of America's new era of close elections.

Two years later, Newt Gingrich led Republicans to their first House majority in thirty-eight years—only the second since 1928.[302] To make it happen, he shrewdly acknowledged the trust gap by requiring candidates to sign the *Contract with America*: a written pledge to vote on ten specific reforms if elected. It nationalized the campaign and gave voters clarity about what a GOP Congress would do.

Still, conservative skepticism toward establishment Republicans never faded. Grover Norquist built a career around extracting *no-new-taxes* pledges from candidates—and holding them accountable if they broke their word.[303]

The 2010 midterms were another watershed. Riding a Tea Party wave and a promise to repeal and replace Obamacare, Republicans won their largest congressional majority in eight decades.[304] Once again, however, GOP voters were disappointed. Many began asking why they should bother voting for Republicans if their representatives simply went to Washington and governed like Democrats.

By 2012, the trust divide inside the GOP was impossible to ignore. Establishment leaders fretted about the passion of Tea Party conservatives—the very voters who had handed them their majority. Party insiders worried that if an establishment candidate like Mitt

---

301 Katherine Q. Seelye, John DiStaso, Star Reporter of New Hampshire Primaries, Dies at 68, *New York Times,* April 28, 2022.

302 "Party Divisions of the House of Representatives, 1789 to Present," History, Art & Archives, US House of Representatives, accessed December 12, 2025, https://history.house.gov/Institution/Party-Divisions/Party-Divisions/.

303 Chris Good, "Norquist's Tax Pledge: What It Is and How It Started," ABC News, November 26, 2012, https://abcnews.go.com/blogs/politics/2012/11/norquists-tax-pledge-what-it-is-and-how-it-started.

304 "Party Divisions."

Romney won the nomination, conservatives who had backed Newt Gingrich or Rick Santorum might sulk and stay home in November.

But this was yet another case of GOP leadership misunderstanding their base. My polling showed the opposite: Tea Party voters were determined to vote against Barack Obama, no matter who the Republican nominee was.[305] The real weak link was establishment Republicans. Romney supporters were far more likely to walk away if a more conservative candidate captured the nomination.

The stage was nearly set for the Trump era.

The final piece of the puzzle came in the form of a Republican National Committee "autopsy" on the party's 2012 defeat. Among its key recommendations: Stop talking about restricting immigration.[306] The RNC's call to retreat on immigration showed just how badly Republican leaders misunderstood their own voters. Donald Trump was about to teach them the cost of that mistake.

---

[305] Polling conducted by the author.

[306] "RNC Completes 'Autopsy' on 2012 Loss, Calls for Inclusion Not Policy Change," ABC News, March 18, 2013, https://abcnews.go.com/Politics/OTUS/rnc-completes-autopsy-2012-loss-calls-inclusion-policy/story?id=18755809.

Chapter 13

THE REAL ENEMY

In 2016, for the first time in modern history, most voters held negative views of both major-party nominees. Hillary Clinton was viewed favorably by just 42 percent of voters and unfavorably by 54 percent. Donald Trump's numbers were slightly worse—38 percent favorable, 59 percent unfavorable.[307]

That both parties nominated such unpopular candidates was a damning indictment of America's broken political system.

Still, Democratic elites rallied behind their candidate despite her deep unpopularity. Outgoing President Obama even declared there had never been a "more qualified" candidate for the presidency.[308]

Republican elites reacted far differently. They dismissed Trump as a buffoonish, unserious candidate destined to lose. They mocked "those garish hats brandishing his provincial slogan, 'Make America

[307] "Election 2016 Favorability Ratings," RealClear Politics, accessed December 12, 2025, https://www.realclearpolitics.com/epolls/other/president/clinton-trumpfavorability.html.

[308] A. J. Chavar and Ben Laffin, "Obama: Nobody 'More Qualified' Than Clinton," *The New York Times*, July 28, 2016, https://www.nytimes.com/video/us/politics/100000004556147/obama-nobody-more-qualified-than-clinton.html.

Great Again.'"[309] They were especially horrified by his blunt talk on immigration—precisely because it ran against the consensus of party leaders, who believed the GOP needed to soften its stance.

In what has been aptly called the "Revolt of the Conservative Elites," Republican leaders did more than bad-mouth their nominee. Every candidate Trump defeated in the primaries had signed a pledge to support whoever won. The pledge was designed to box Trump in, ensuring he wouldn't run as a third-party spoiler. But when he emerged as the nominee, several rivals broke their word—including Ohio Governor John Kasich, businesswoman Carly Fiorina, and former Florida Governor Jeb Bush.[310]

That rejection among Republican political pros was only the tip of the iceberg. Neither George H. W. Bush nor George W. Bush voted for Trump.[311] The two previous GOP presidential nominees—Mitt Romney and John McCain—publicly opposed him.[312] Nearly a dozen sitting Republican senators, along with a comparable number of governors, joined the anti-Trump chorus. The roster of

---

[309] Robert P. Saldin and Steven M. Teles, *Never Trump* (Oxford University Press: 2020), p. 1.

[310] November 6, 2016, "The Republicans Opposing Donald Trump — And Voting for Hillary Clinton", NBC News https://www.nbcnews.com/politics/2016-election/meet-republicans-speaking-out-against-trump-n530696

[311] November 4, 2017, "George Bush Sr calls Trump a 'blowhard' and voted for Clinton", BBC

[312] November 6, 2016, "The Republicans Opposing Donald Trump — And Voting for Hillary Clinton", NBC News https://www.nbcnews.com/politics/2016-election/meet-republicans-speaking-out-against-trump-n530696.

congressmen and former GOP officials who distanced themselves from their party's nominee was longer still.[313]

Hillary Clinton had lived in the White House, served as a US senator, and been secretary of state. Her résumé, demeanor, and elite-friendly worldview made her the dream candidate of the Political Class. Even many Republican insiders regarded her as a fellow member of their club—a club that would never admit someone like Donald Trump.

For many in the GOP establishment, Clinton's progressive worldview was easier to accept than Trump's populism. That revealed how thoroughly the Wilsonian model—largely advanced by progressive elites in universities, media, and bureaucracy—had seeped into the Republican establishment itself.

Few of these leaders imagined that Trump, who had never held elected office, could actually win.

On Election Day, just 38 percent of voters believed Donald Trump was qualified to serve as president, and only 35 percent thought he had the right temperament for the job. Those were precisely the numbers political elites in both parties expected.[314]

What they never anticipated was that millions would vote for Trump despite doubting his qualifications. In fact, while only 38 percent considered him qualified, 46 percent still cast their ballots for him.[315] That meant roughly eleven million Americans knowingly chose a man they believed unqualified—an unmistakable sign of how deeply frustrated voters had become with an unresponsive government.

---

[313] August 29, 2016, "More Than160 Republican Leaders Don't Support Donald Trump", *The New York Times,* https://www.nytimes.com/interactive/2016/08/29/us/politics/at-least-110-republican-leaders-wont-vote-for-donald-trump-heres-when-they-reached-their-breaking-point.html

[314] CNN Exit polls, https://www.cnn.com/election/2016/results/exit-polls.

[315] Ibid.

The meaning of this was not immediately clear, but it was obvious that something big, unusual, and important had occurred. In *Star Wars* terms, there was a tremor in the Force.

The election results were more than a personal rejection of Hillary Clinton. To many voters, she embodied the Political Class itself. That was a big negative in an election where voters were more interested in a candidate who could bring change rather than for someone with the right experience or good judgement.[316] Voting against Clinton was a way of voting against the elite political world she represented.

For elites, the election of Donald Trump was an unforgivable mistake. It reinforced their Wilsonian conviction that ordinary Americans were too ignorant to govern themselves. In their eyes, the people had put an "outrageous outsider" in charge.

From the moment he was elected, Trump faced an unprecedented level of bipartisan resistance in both the federal bureaucracy and larger policy circles. Much of this resistance was driven by institutions already dominated by the left—federal agencies, universities, media outlets, and cultural gatekeepers. However, offended by their party's candidate and the base that voted for him, many Republican elites joined the resistance as well.

As political scientists Robert Saldin and Steven Teles observed, no modern Western party had ever sought to govern while facing such an extraordinary level of intraparty opposition. The "white-hot core" of the resistance to Trump came not from voters but from professionals, public intellectuals, operatives, and once-and-future political appointees—the very network modern parties rely on to staff and sustain government.[317]

Trump himself was unprepared for what awaited him. He reportedly did not realize how many key posts he would need to fill, and

---

[316] Ibid.

[317] Saldin and Teles, *Never Trump*, p.4

he lacked an established network of policy experts to draw upon.[318] Rather than help, many conservative elites inside government and policy circles joined Democrats in mounting bipartisan resistance to his administration.

Many pre-Trump Republican leaders told professors Saldin and Teles that they "had an obligation to help save their party and the country from what they saw as the worst instincts of their own base."[319] They opposed Trump precisely because he was willing to fight for what the base wanted—rather than what elites deemed acceptable. In their eyes, his gravest sin was "giving the party's voters what they wanted rather than what party leaders thought acceptable to give them."[320]

By refusing to help President Trump, elite Republican leaders may have believed the chaos they helped create would eventually teach voters a lesson. But it didn't work out that way. As 2020 began, Trump was clearly favored to win reelection.

Then came the COVID-19 pandemic. Businesses shuttered, forty million Americans lost their jobs, and Trump fell short in his reelection bid. Wilsonian elitists assumed they had survived the storm. They could not imagine voters ever returning Trump to the White House—especially after the way he contested the outcome.

But Trump did return, and stronger than before. He may not have fully grasped the political game in his first term, but he proved to be a fast learner. Over four years in the political wilderness, he studied his missteps, built a network, and prepared for a comeback. Organizations like the America First Policy Institute (AFPI) helped shape policy ideas, refine an agenda, and assemble a team ready to govern from day one.

---

[318] Ibid, p. 4.
[319] Ibid, p. 6.
[320] Ibid, p 5.

When he returned, Trump not only understood the political game—he played it better than many of his opponents. As Bruce Mehlman observed, "Trump 2.0 is operating with broader ambitions, more fearlessness & greater understanding of how to maneuver the levers of power."[321]

The difference showed immediately. In his opening days back in office, Trump signed dozens of executive orders, fulfilling campaign promises with broad popular support. These included making English the official language of the United States, banning biological males from competing in women's sports, eliminating government censorship programs, and more.[322]

Looking back, Trump's four years in exile left him better prepared to transform the federal bureaucracy than he could have been had he won in 2020.

The old Republican policy elites had been pushed aside, and Trump began his second term with allies inside the bureaucracy. A Napolitan Institute survey found that 44 percent of federal government managers planned to support his efforts.[323] That support was reinforced by Cabinet members and political appointees committed to the America First agenda who had spent four years readying for a new term.

Resistance did not vanish, but it took a new shape. While 44 percent of managers planned to support the president, 42 percent planned to resist. For the first time, a partisan battle was playing out inside the leadership ranks of the bureaucracy itself:

- Eighty-nine percent of Republican managers said they would support the Trump administration.

---

[321] Bruce Mehlman, "Six-Chart Sunday, Decoding Trump 2.0," *Bruce Mehlman's Age of Disruption*, December 14, 2025

[322] "Elite 1 Percent."

[323] Napolitan Institute, *The Resistance: The First 100 Days.*

- Seventy-three percent of Democratic managers said they intended to resist.[324]

On one level, such a divide is unsurprising in a nation already consumed by hyper-partisan conflict. But the Napolitan survey revealed something more troubling. Asked what they would do if they disagreed with a direct, legal order from the president, only 16 percent of managers who had voted for Kamala Harris said they would follow it. Seventy-five percent said they would ignore it.[325] So much for Woodrow Wilson's assurance that administrators would have nothing to do with politics.

Trump's second term thus marked a seismic shift in the behavior of the federal bureaucracy. Before his rise, government officials at least nominally supported presidents of both parties. After his first victory, the political establishment circled the wagons to mount bipartisan resistance. By his second term, the bureaucracy had become a fully partisan battleground.

The partisan split among federal managers now mirrored the public at large. Seventy-nine percent of Republican managers believed cutting government spending was good for the economy, while 70 percent of Democratic managers said it was bad. During debate over making Trump's tax cuts permanent, 92 percent of Republican managers supported it, compared to 78 percent of Democrats who opposed it.[326]

Whatever else Trump accomplished, he had transformed the federal bureaucracy from a body that once lent some measure of support to presidents of either party into a hyper-partisan arena.

That wasn't the only transformation in recent political history. Something significant had happened to the movement President

---

324 Ibid.

325 Ibid.

326 Ibid.

George H. W. Bush inadvertently unleashed when he broke his "no new taxes" pledge. At first, it was little more than a cry for government to listen and remember who was in charge. Over time—especially during the Tea Party era—it hardened into an angrier political force. Trump's election in 2016 brought a fleeting victory, followed by even deeper outrage at the establishment's organized resistance.

By Trump's second term, the MAGA movement had become a political army—equal and opposite to the mobilized army of the political left. Whatever the issue, both partisan camps were now quick to switch positions if it meant scoring a point for their side.

Democrats who once railed against the Supreme Court for blocking President Biden's student loan forgiveness plan now condemned Trump for disregarding judicial authority. Republicans who denounced Biden's sweeping executive orders turned around and cheered just as loudly when Trump issued orders they favored.

Rather than dismantle Wilsonian government by unelected elites, Trump's second administration simply placed it under new management. His supporters had no interest in shrinking government power. Quite the opposite: They applauded him for wielding it in their cause.

In today's terms, Trump's political army was fighting the political army of the New Left—the elites determined to reshape America's culture. The MAGA base saw itself in direct combat with what they called the "woke progressive army." They cheered loudly when Trump banned biological males from competing in women's sports, seeing such victories as proof that he was using every available lever of government to wage their cultural war.

The more the partisan political armies got caught up fighting each other, the less they thought about representing the 80 percent who don't want to be ruled from the left, the right, or even the center. The political warriors lost touch with the Midwestern women and millions like them who want to govern their own lives, raise their families, enjoy their friends and neighbors, and build better communities.

Watching that unfold, I finally understood why it had been so hard to identify the real enemy. In the first three *Hunger Games* films, the real enemy seemed obvious: it was the ruthless Capitol leader, President Snow. Life was good for the wealthy Capitol elite who supported Snow and lived off the labor of the oppressed districts. The comparison with official Washington was obvious, if a bit exaggerated.

In the movies, most people in the outlying districts were unhappy but resigned — convinced there was nothing they could do. Once again, the comparison with our recent history seemed clear: millions of Americans have become justifiably frustrated with our unresponsive political system. Many have given up hope of ever being heard. To them, the enemy seemed clear: it was the corrupt Capitol system run by politicians and bureaucrats.

As the movie storyline progressed, however, the audience learned about a surprising source of hope—District 13. Most Panem residents thought the district had long ago been destroyed by the Capitol. In reality, the survivors of the Capitol attack simply went underground and quietly assembled a powerful army. Eventually, the District 13 army was unleashed and rallied the nation to fight the distant Capitol. Ordinary citizens didn't know much about District 13, but they knew who it was fighting against.

In a similar vein, millions of Americans voted for Donald Trump in 2016 despite thinking he was unqualified for the job and not being sure about much of his agenda. What they did know, however, is who he was fighting against. That was enough.

A plot twist in the movie series' final film raised surprising questions about who the real enemy was. It turned out that District 13's leader, President Coin, was not really interested in a free Panem. She simply wanted to win the power to run the Capitol herself. The lesson was clear: the real enemy was not Snow or Coin, but the Capitol system that enriched and empowered them. The corrupt system itself was the problem, the real enemy.

From this perspective, President Trump might best be described as the president of District 13. He tapped into the very real frustrations of the American people on issues official Washington had long ignored. In doing so, he gained power and blew up the cozy Wilsonian system run by establishment Republicans and Democrats alike.

However, once in office, President Trump enjoyed using the power of Wilsonian government every bit as much as Presidents Obama and Biden had done. Just like his predecessors, Trump wanted to unilaterally impose his vision on the nation and showed little patience for anything that got in his way. Politicians always believe checks and balances are vitally important when the other team is in power, but both teams also believe things should be different when they are in charge.

This change in perspective is not at all unusual. Thomas Jefferson, drafter of the Declaration of Independence and our third president, had been a huge fan of voluntary, self-governing societies when the British were in charge of colonial America. As he put it, such associations had been necessary when "the government had combined against the rights of the people."

Jefferson, however, changed his tune after the colonists won their Independence and he became part of the government. All of a sudden, he "feared that the proliferation of voluntary associations would lead again to revolution, this time against legitimate republican governments."[327] In other words, things are different when my team is in charge. Human nature never changes.

---

[327] Elisabeth S. Clemens and Doug Guthrie, Politics and Partnerships: The Role of Voluntary Associations in America's Political Past and Present, (Chicago: University of Chicago Press, 2011), 3

With Trump in office, the focus of his army shifted as well. For some of his most ardent supporters, defeating the New Left became all that mattered. "If the Right doesn't use force back against the Left, then America is done for," according to a social media response attacking my commitment to our nation's founding ideals. Another added "Consent of the governed??? We're not liberals, Scott."

Notre Dame professor Patrick Deneen wrote that such attitudes reflect a "widespread yearning for a strong leader." Deneen, who openly rejects America's founding ideals, is thinking of a leader who will "take back popular control of bureaucratized government."[328]

Rather than looking to unwind government by the unelected, they simply want to find the "right" person to wield the power. Vocal Trump supporter Laura Loomer personified this attitude in a particularly dramatic manner by declaring "I want a King."[329]

Talk about un-American!

Such views come from being seduced by the real enemy, the corrupt Wilsonian system of government that grants presidents and unelected officials far too much power over everyday life. It is not only corrupt, but corrupting — seductive enough to ensnare even the purest of hearts and the best of intentions.

The only way to defeat that enemy is to restore a self-governing society.

Unfortunately, the fog of war created by the two armies makes it hard to see clearly how to proceed. As a first step, the 80 percent must recognize that the real enemy is not President Trump, President Biden, President Obama, or any group of shadowy figures. It is the Wilsonian system of government itself.

That distinction matters, because while only a small fraction of Americans are caught up in the political war, their behavior

---

[328] Patrick, Deneen *Why Liberalism Failed,* (Yale University Press, 2017)
[329] https://x.com/LauraLoomer/status/1993823372590100944

increasingly defines the system the rest of us must live under. The 80 percent may want to raise families, build communities, and live freely, but their future is often limited or attacked by the 20 percent locked in partisan combat. And the more these rival armies fight, the more they create a culture of dependency that leaves voters sidelined and frustrated.

Chapter 14

A CULTURE OF DEPENDENCY

The hyper-partisan behavior of federal managers thrills the small slice of Americans most invested in partisan warfare. These activists celebrate even the smallest victories over the other side and vow revenge when they lose. They get an adrenaline rush from "owning" opponents on social media or winning the daily news cycle.

But only about 10 percent of Americans on the far left (progressive activists) and another 10 percent on the far right (MAGA loyalists) are caught up in this game. For the other 80 percent—like the two Midwestern women we've met—the spectacle looks childish and exhausting. They believe government leaders should listen to and represent voters. Instead, they see politicians serving Team Red or Team Blue, ignoring constituents, and playing petty games.

There is some good news. Whenever elites are locked in combat, openings emerge for other voices to be heard. That's true in all societies and organizations. As we'll see later, the partisan stalemate within government may provide opportunities to move decision-making closer to home and restore America's founding ideal of self-governance.

The bad news is that the dysfunction and partisanship of Washington harms the entire nation. One of the clearest examples can be found in today's higher-education culture wars.

Beginning in the 1960s, the federal government replaced private student loans with federally backed loans. Today, colleges and universities take in more than $80 billion a year from the federal loan program.[330] Only a handful of schools, such as Hillsdale College, refuse to accept the money.

For most schools, the program was like manna from heaven. More students could afford to attend, tuition kept climbing, and administrators could hire more faculty and staff. What wasn't to like? All they had to do was play by Washington's rules.

Those rules changed dramatically over time. In 1972, Title IX required schools to eliminate sex-based discrimination. One important benefit was the dramatic growth of women's sports. (On a personal note, I was an unintended beneficiary: Umpiring women's fast-pitch softball games at the college level helped me pay the bills.)

But starting decades later, progressive administrations used Title IX as a tool to impose sweeping cultural changes. In 2011, the Obama administration redefined *sex* to mean gender identity rather than biological sex. Colleges were told to let students use bathrooms aligned with their gender identity.

When Trump took office, that interpretation was overturned, restoring the law's original meaning: males in the men's room, females in the women's. But four years later, the Biden administration flipped the policy again, requiring schools to allow biological males to compete in women's sports if they identified as female. That progressive mandate sparked a national uproar and helped fuel Republican gains in the 2024 elections.

When Trump returned for a second term, the rules flipped once more. Colleges were ordered to ban biological males from women's sports. Each shift triggered new lawsuits.

---

[330] Melanie Hanson, "Financial Aid Statistics," Education Data Initiative, last updated February 3, 2025, https://educationdata.org/financial-aid-statistics.

This kind of whiplash—rules changing every four years at the stroke of a presidential pen—is unhealthy for any society. It reflects the deeper reality of Wilsonian government: Progressives advance expansive interpretations of federal power, and conservatives are left either to fight back with the same tools or watch cultural norms be rewritten from Washington. Worse still, the nation's entire approach to education policy could shift yet again in 2028, depending on how a few thousand voters in a handful of swing states cast their ballots.

Former Secretary of State Henry Kissinger once described US–Soviet relations during the Cold War as "two heavily armed blind men feeling their way around a room, each believing himself in mortal peril from the other."[331] Both political teams today project the same mindset, warning their followers that civilization itself will collapse if they lose the next election. That's why, like clockwork, every cycle brings a flood of columns and TV segments insisting this is "the most important election of our lifetime." The phrase has been repeated so often—for midterms as well as presidential races—that it has lost all meaning, even as it keeps ratcheting up public fear.

The danger, as Kissinger added, is that "over time, even two armed blind men can do enormous damage to each other—not to speak of the room."[332] This is no way to run a government. It is precisely the kind of politics America's early colonists sought to escape.

Consider England in the sixteenth and seventeenth centuries. The Catholic–Protestant struggle was every bit as fierce as today's transgender debates. When Pope Clement VII refused to annul Henry VIII's marriage to Anne Boleyn, the king broke with Rome, established the Church of England, and named himself its head. His

---

[331] David Cohen, "Henry Kissinger, diplomat who helped to reshape the world, dies at 100," *Politico*, November 29, 2023, https://www.politico.com/news/2023/11/29/henry-kissinger-diplomat-nobel-obituary-031478.

[332] Ibid.

new rules required citizens to worship on the king's terms, and penalties for dissent were severe.

A generation later, Henry's daughter, Mary Tudor, reversed course, restoring Catholicism as England's official faith. Her brutal enforcement of the new order earned her the name "Bloody Mary," as hundreds of Protestants were burned at the stake. After her death, the crown reversed direction again, reinstating Anglican worship and persecuting Catholics and other dissenters.

This endless cycle of decree and retribution—religious policy dictated from the throne—eventually drove the Puritans to flee England for Massachusetts. They longed for a system not defined by royal mandates but by the freedom to govern their own communities.

As described earlier, the desire to escape the tyranny of a king-mandated religion also led to the illegal founding of Harvard. The importance of that moment is hard to overstate. The colonists realized they could form organizations of every kind without asking permission from the Crown. By decoupling their society from royal authority, they were no longer dependent on it.

The Crown recognized this far too late. Much of the decade leading up to the Revolution was the monarchy's desperate attempt to reassert control. Each effort was met with colonial resistance.

In 1773, for example, the king decreed that colonial judges would no longer be paid by the colonies.[333] Frustrated that judges were not doing enough to rein in "rebels," he wanted them dependent on him alone. Rule against the Crown, and you could lose your job.

Colonial leaders were outraged—so much so that this grievance made its way into the Declaration of Independence: "He has made Judges dependent on his Will alone." The king—not colonial

---

[333] Steven H. Aden, "Accountability of Judges, and the Declaration of Independence," Constituting America, accessed December 12, 2025, https://constitutingamerica.org/90day-dcin-accountability-of-judges-and-the-declaration-of-independence-guest-essayist-steven-h-aden.

governments—would decide "the tenure of their offices, and the amount and payment of their salaries."

Over the past century and a half, believers in Wilsonian government have acted much the same way. Like King George, they have sought to coopt large segments of American society by making them dependent on federal largesse. And while both parties have contributed, the steady expansion of federal programs has been overwhelmingly driven by progressive elites who view Washington as the rightful center of authority.

Today, Washington provides more than $1 trillion each year to state and local governments.[334] Voters may elect mayors and governors, but those leaders know their survival depends on the paymaster in Washington.

Billions more flow to "charitable" nongovernmental organizations (NGOs), many with little oversight or accountability. Often these groups operate as slush funds for the politically connected. Many receive more money from government than they raise from private contributions. Most voters have little knowledge of NGOs, but when the idea is explained in neutral terms, half of Americans say such groups should not be eligible for federal funding.[335]

Corporate America is equally ensnared. Companies compete for contracts, favorable regulations, and tax breaks, with around twelve thousand registered lobbyists spending more than $4 billion a year seeking favors.[336] The real numbers are almost certainly higher.

Why do companies invest so much in lobbyists? Brookings scholar Jonathan Rauch quoted a Washington lobbyist who admitted, "If I throw in a million here or a million there, I might get

---

[334] "Federal Grants to State and Local Governments: Trends and Issues," .gov, June 26, 2025, https://www.congress.gov/crs-product/R40638.

[335] Dec 3–4, 2024, Napolitan News data from survey of 1,000 registered voters

[336] Abigail Tierney, "Lobbying in the U.S.—statistics & facts," Statista, February 25, 2025, https://www.statista.com/topics/11840/lobbying-in-the-us/#topicOverview.

a hundred million back."[337] The lobbyist, a former congressional staffer, added, "And there are probably enough cases like that so they keep throwing money in."

The result is a nation where major institutions have grown dependent on federal dollars and the bureaucrats who control them. Rauch calls it the "parasite economy." By coopting universities, NGOs, corporations, and state governments—and by insulating officials from voter accountability—Wilsonian idealists have come dangerously close to snuffing out the ability of ordinary Americans to control their government.

Seen in this light, the hyper-partisan divide among federal managers looks even more ominous. The two teams are not battling over how best to represent voters—or even over which voters to represent. They are fighting for control of the vast power and money that flow so that they can keep American society dependent on their side.

What's most troubling is not what divides these managers, but what unites them. Across party lines, an uncomfortably large number embrace the core assumptions of Wilsonian government.

- Thirty-nine percent of government managers—37 percent of Republicans and 42 percent of Democrats—say America would be better off if only college graduates could vote.[338]
- When asked how to handle a conflict between their own views and what voters want, most (54 percent) said they would ignore the voters and do what they think is right. That includes 49 percent of Republican managers and 60 percent of Democrats.[339]

---

[337] Jonathan Rauch, *Government's End: Why Washington Stopped Working* (PublicAffairs: 1999).

[338] May 1–15, 2024—Napolitan Institute data from survey of 504 federal government managers.

[339] Napolitan Institute, "Elite 1 Percent."

It's not hard to see how this mindset takes root. Those who see themselves as experts naturally assume their judgment is superior to that of the public. They've studied the issue, earned credentials, and invested years in government service. And in Washington's political culture, it is often considered a badge of honor to "stand up to the voters"—especially when doing so advances government by the unelected.

Whatever the reasoning, it is impossible to square that elitist attitude with the founding belief that government derives its only legitimate authority from the consent of the governed.

The perception gap between the American people and unelected federal officials is enormous. Voters don't trust government and consistently want less of it. By a two-to-one margin, they say less government control and regulation would be good for the economy.

Federal managers—Republican and Democrat alike—take the opposite view. They are more likely to trust government and to distrust voters. They have convinced themselves that unelected officials in Washington know better than families in America's heartland. As a result, most Republican managers (55 percent) and most Democratic managers (51 percent) say the economy would perform better with more government control.[340]

In practice, both political teams inside the bureaucracy assume the economy would thrive if their team were in charge. But on the more fundamental question—should Americans govern themselves?—both sides are dismissive. This bipartisan elitism shows up again and again in the data:

- Censorship: Forty-eight percent of Democratic managers believe the government should be able to censor social media posts. So do 53 percent of Republican managers.[341]

[340] Napolitan Institute, *Resistance Report*.

[341] Ibid.

- Parental rights: Half of Democratic managers (50 percent) say parents have too much control over their children's education. So do 42 percent of Republican managers. Hardly anyone in Washington thinks parents have too little control.[342]
- Guns: In a striking display of consensus, 79 percent of Democratic managers and 74 percent of Republican managers favor banning private gun ownership.[343]

On every point, the American people strongly disagree.

These findings paint a chilling portrait of the hyper-partisan battle raging within the federal bureaucracy. The competing teams may want to take the country in different directions, but they share a dangerous conviction: Power belongs to whichever side wins the partisan game. If we lose, the other team will rewrite society's rules. If we win, we'll rewrite them back.

Who cares about freedom, equality, or self-governance when you can force America's most powerful institutions to obey your commands?

The uncomfortable reality is that Wilsonian elitists, from both parties, view the restoration of America's founding ideals as an existential threat. Woodrow Wilson himself once complained that "some citizens of this country have never got beyond the Declaration of Independence."[344]

That is the voice of the Elitist Revolt. People who share Wilson's dream have little interest in surrendering the power and money that flow from today's dependency system. They take challenges to their authority personally and lash out at voters who still believe in the founding ideals. Their anger at the public is not incidental—it

342 Ibid.

343 May 1–15, 2024—Napolitan Institute data from survey of 504 federal government managers.

344 The New Freedom. https://constitutioncenter.org/the-constitution/historic-document-library/detail/woodrow-wilson-the-new-freedom-1913

has become the root cause of the hateful, toxic tone that defines twenty-first-century American politics.

Anger at voters may explain the tone of American politics, but it doesn't explain the scale of the corruption. To see that, we must look at how Washington has become the hub of a vast "parasite economy"—an exchange where the true currency is insider privilege.

Chapter 15

THE 519,000

The federal government today is the hub of what Brookings Institution scholar Jonathan Rauch once called the "parasite economy." He described it as "a New York Stock Exchange on which government benefits are sought and traded openly and (for the most part) honestly."[345]

That last qualifier—"for the most part"—may be generous. After all, those who benefit most from the system are the same ones who write the rules governing it. Members of Congress, for example, are legally permitted to trade individual stocks while in office. Many seem to possess an uncanny knack for buying or selling shares just before major news breaks. Their timing is often so precise that ordinary investors could be forgiven for wondering if the game is rigged.

It's no wonder that 64 percent of voters believe members of Congress should be banned from trading stocks while in office.[346] Like Wall Street itself, Washington's "exchange" is technically open to everyone—but it works best for the elites and insiders who know how to play the system.

---

[345] Rauch, *Government's End.*

[346] April 16, 2025—Napolitan News data from survey of 1,000 registered voters.

Even more troubling, this parasite economy encourages large corporations to "invest" in lobbyists rather than expand their businesses. Winning a tax break or hobbling a competitor can be far more profitable than hiring workers or developing new products. Everyday Americans may not follow the details, but 63 percent of voters understand that big government and big business often work together in ways that harm consumers and small businesses.[347]

The result is a lucrative market for influence. Rauch observed that "government itself becomes a marketable resource and a profit center for an expanding group of career-minded professionals."[348] Many of those professionals use government jobs as steppingstones to high-paying careers lobbying the very institutions they once served.

This is the natural result of concentrating power and giving unelected officials sweeping authority. That pattern has existed since the creation of the very first federal regulatory agency in 1887. The Interstate Commerce Commission (ICC) was established to regulate the railroads—but the agency was quickly captured by the industry it was meant to oversee. Instead of protecting the public, it shielded the railroads from competition and enriched them at the public's expense.

Nearly a century later, when President Jimmy Carter deregulated the industry, the scale of that enrichment became clear. In 1980, writes Rauch, "shippers saved as much as $5 billion a year" once the ICC's rules were lifted—a sum equivalent to about $20 billion a year today.[349] In effect, the ICC had been making the railroads, their lobbyists, and their political allies richer by $5 billion annually while making everyone else poorer by the same amount.

The railroads were not unique. I began flying for business shortly before the airlines were deregulated in 1978. Back then, air travel was

---

[347] April 14–15, 2025—Napolitan News data from survey of 1,000 registered voters.

[348] Rauch, *Government's End.*

[349] Ibid.

comfortable but costly: great service, full meals, and plenty of empty seats. After deregulation, the cost of flying dropped by more than 20 percent, passenger volume doubled, and airline safety improved dramatically.[350]

Regulation had been good for the airlines and for those of us whose companies picked up the bill. It was also good for many of the players in the parasite economy who profited from federal control. But removing those regulatory "parasites" proved far better for everyone else.

Most Americans view the parasite economy with disgust. When Gallup measured the perceived ethical standards of various occupations, members of Congress and lobbyists rated lower than any other profession.[351] In sharp contrast, many of those inside it see their work as entirely normal—even virtuous. They justify their efforts by claiming to represent worthy causes: the poor, the elderly, national security, or civil rights.

Many of these players bristle at the idea that people across the country see them as corrupt or self-interested. "Washington is not a cynical swamp," a *Washington Post* headline once insisted. It is "America's most hopeful place…a city full of idealists who persist in the belief that they can make a difference."[352]

Anyone who believes that glowing image of official Washington has embraced Woodrow Wilson's dream. So have the many who may be more pragmatic but remain invested in keeping the system alive. Having bought into the system, they have no more interest

---

[350] Ibid.

[351] Lydia Saad, "Americans' Ratings of U.S. Professions Stay Historically Low," Gallup, January 13, 2025, https://news.gallup.com/poll/655106/americans-ratings-professions-stay-historically-low.aspx.

[352] David Litt, "Washington, D.C., is not a cynical swamp. It's America's most hopeful place," October 5, 2017, https://www.washingtonpost.com/news/posteverything/wp/2017/10/05/washington-d-c-is-not-a-cynical-swamp-its-americas-most-hopeful-place/.

in restoring America's founding ideals than the Montgomery City Council once had in ending segregation.

That is a hard reality for most Americans to accept.

This means that, as bad as things were for Dr. King and his followers in 1955, they had one crucial advantage over most Americans today—they understood what they were up against. They knew that Montgomery's leaders rejected the very notion that the city's Black citizens deserved equality. By facing that truth squarely, they were able to develop a winning strategy.

To develop a strategy for ending the elitist revolt, we must first understand what we are up against. Leaders of the Wilsonian government—on both sides of the political aisle—reject the very idea of a self-governing society. Some oppose it for ideological reasons, others because the current system serves them well. Still others have simply been seduced by the parasite economy and the comforting illusion that what's good for Washington must be good for America.

Whatever their motives, we must recognize that official Washington has become the central hub of the elitist revolt against America's founding ideals. It is fueled by the parasite economy, justified by Wilsonian theories of rule by "experts," and sustained through a dense web of powerful institutions.

That web includes corporations, banks, investment firms, insurance companies, media empires, the White House, Congress, the federal bureaucracy, prestigious law firms, and high-powered lobbyists. Political scientist Thomas Dye—who argues that roughly four thousand elites determine how the rest of us live—adds to that list "fat cat political contributors, foundations, universities, and private policy planning organizations."[353]

That is why we need the kind of leadership Dr. King modeled in Montgomery and beyond, right up until the day he was assassinated. The leadership America needs now must understand that we can't

[353] Dye, *Who's Running America?*

outbid lobbyists or reform Washington from within. That game is rigged. Real change will not come from playing it better—but from refusing to play it at all.

The good news is that nearly every major movement for progress in American history has begun far from the halls of power.

For forty years, beginning in 1878, Congress repeatedly voted against granting women the right to vote. One of the most powerful forces opposing suffrage was the liquor industry. Susan B. Anthony and other leaders saw a "natural alliance" between the suffrage movement and the temperance movement: Empower women to vote so they could protect their homes and families by placing legal limits on liquor.[354] The liquor industry, fearing that female voters would push for prohibition, lobbied aggressively to keep women from the polls.

Had suffragists relied solely on lobbying Congress, women might never have gained the right to vote.

Instead, the movement's leaders got creative. They decided to work around Congress, focusing on the states. One by one, they persuaded individual states to extend the vote to women—recognizing that each state had unique political conditions and that states competed with one another to attract new residents.

In 1911, for instance, a quarter of a million California men voted on a ballot initiative to decide whether women should be allowed to vote. According to the secretary of state's office, "the measure was soundly defeated in the San Francisco Bay Area and just barely passed in Los Angeles."[355] But votes "in the rural districts successfully

---

[354] Elaine Weiss, "Women, Booze, and the Vote," *The New York Times*, March 5, 2018, https://www.nytimes.com/2018/03/05/opinion/women-votes-feminism-alcohol.html.

[355] Robert P. J. Cooney, Jr, "A Brief Summary of the 1911 Campaign," California Women Suffrage Centennial, California Secretary of State, https://www.sos.ca.gov/elections/celebrating-womens-suffrage/california-women-suffrage-centennial.

overcame the more organized opposition in the cities." The initiative passed by a razor-thin 50.7 percent.

Why did urban Californians resist while rural voters embraced the idea? The difference came down largely to values and alliances. Rural communities had stronger church networks and closer ties to both the temperance and suffrage movements. Urban voters were more aligned with liquor interests. In other words, suffragists succeeded by framing the issue in a way that aligned women's rights with the self-interest of rural men.

The state-by-state approach worked so well that a woman, Jeannette Rankin, was elected to represent Montana in Congress before Congress itself had voted to let women vote. Once her state extended suffrage, she became eligible for office. One can only imagine the reaction in the Capitol the day she arrived to take her seat.

Ultimately, it was not congressional persuasion that delivered women the vote but creative persistence outside Washington. Once enough states had acted, Congress had no choice but to follow.

A similar lesson guided the term-limits movement of the early 1990s. Expecting members of Congress to impose limits on themselves, as I used to say, "was like expecting a toddler to set a reasonable bedtime for himself." Given that reality, creative workarounds were essential.

Reading the Constitution, leaders of the term-limits movement concluded that states had the authority to set limits on their own congressional delegations. Acting on that belief, we launched a state-by-state campaign to bypass Congress and impose term limits through state law. The movement succeeded in enacting limits of three terms in the House (six years) and two in the Senate (twelve years) across twenty-three states. Nearly half of Congress was effectively term-limited.

Then, in a narrow five to four decision, the Supreme Court struck down the effort.[356] The ruling overturned the will of millions of voters and freed members of Congress from the limits their own states had imposed.

That setback was disappointing—but it also offered a valuable lesson. Even when Washington resists reform, meaningful change can still begin outside it.

Today, there are 519,000 state and local elected officials serving in one of 87,576 governing bodies across America.

- 7,383 state legislators serve in ninety-nine legislative chambers (every state but Nebraska has two).
- More than fifty-eight thousand officials serve in roughly three thousand county governments.[357]
- Tens of thousands of municipal, town, and township governments are led by more than two hundred fifty thousand elected officials.
- Around ninety-five thousand school board members oversee more than thirteen thousand local districts.
- Thousands more serve in statewide offices, special districts, and other local entities.

Put together, the numbers are staggering: there are nearly a thousand state and local elected officials for every member of Congress.[358]

These 519,000 leaders are the key to restoring America's founding ideals of freedom, equality, and self-governance. They share at least three qualities that make them uniquely important to national renewal.

---

[356] U.S. Term Limits, Inc. v. Thornton, 514 US 779 (1995).

[357] Scott Rasmussen, "Scott Rasmussen's Number of the Day for April 26, 2017," Ballotpedia, https://ballotpedia.org/Scott_Rasmussen%27s_Number_of_the_Day_for_April_26,_2017.

[358] Ibid.

First, they each have a personal following. You can't win even the smallest school board race without supporters behind you. Unlike members of Congress, most local officials know their constituents not as data points in a poll but as neighbors and friends. They hear from them daily—at the grocery store, at church, on the sidelines of youth sports. Collectively, these local leaders embody the voices of ordinary Americans far more authentically than anyone in Washington ever could.

Second, local officials have more influence in Washington than most voters realize. Former US Senator Cory Gardner told me he personally read every letter from local elected officials. He received summaries of phone calls and form letters from other constituents, but messages from local leaders stood out—and were taken seriously.

The ability to stay close to their communities while being heard in the halls of power makes local officials a vital conduit in America's political life. The importance of these conduits can be seen in the very creation of our founding document.

The Declaration of Independence was not drafted by a colonial think tank, ratified by Congress, and handed down to the people as a finished product. It emerged from the ground up. As Rutgers professor David Greenberg observed, Jefferson and the Continental Congress produced their final version after what could fairly be described as an early form of crowdsourcing.

Before Jefferson put pen to parchment, more than one hundred other "declarations of independence" had already been issued by towns, counties, and colonies in the months leading up to July 4, 1776.[359] Many of their ideas and phrases echoed through the final text.

[359] David Greenberg, "America's 100 Other Declarations of Independence," *Politico Magazine*, July 4, 2017, https://www.politico.com/magazine/story/2017/07/04/americas-100-other-declarations-of-independence-215326/.

The Declaration was, in Greenberg's words, "authored not by one man but by a chorus of voices in a fledgling nation whose people had caught independence fever."[360] These local leaders and assemblies "were suddenly proclaiming it with contagious enthusiasm." The principles of freedom, equality, and self-governance did not originate with Jefferson alone—they reflected what he later called "an expression of the American mind."[361]

We need that same kind of bottom-up politics today. A healthy system of self-governance requires state and local officials to find creative ways to make Washington listen—to remind national politicians what is happening in the real America. Too often, federal leaders prefer to lecture, regulate, or reward rather than listen. It falls to the 519,000 to make sure they do.

The third trait all state and local officials share is perhaps the most important. At some point, on some issue, every one of them will have a reason to take power back from the federal government. And almost every local official, sooner or later, will want to take power back from the state government as well.

With this in mind, we should look for creative ways to help the 519,000 state and local officials bring power and decision-making closer to home. This is precisely what the Founding Fathers intended. As James Madison wrote in *The Federalist Papers*, "Ambition must be made to counteract ambition."[362]

The ambition of local leaders may be the most effective force we have to counter the ambition of Washington's parasite economy. Madison understood that was the only way "to control the abuses of government."[363] Each time local officials succeed in shifting authority from the federal government to the states—or from the

---

[360] Ibid.

[361] Ibid.

[362] James Madison and Alexander Hamilton, "Federalist 51."

[363] Ibid.

states to the local level—it represents real progress toward restoring self-governance.

This process will take both patience and discipline. Wilson and his followers have spent nearly 140 years eroding the principles that made America an exceptional nation. Reversing that trend will not happen overnight. It will require what Jonathan Rauch calls "radical incrementalism"—the determination to achieve revolutionary change over the long arc of time. In his words, the goal is "determined, unceasing incremental change."[364]

He's right. But I'd describe radical incrementalism a bit differently.

Losing weight offers a useful analogy. There are two basic approaches. One is to try a crash diet or some overhyped miracle drug. You might shed pounds quickly, but the side effects can be severe—and the results rarely last. The other approach is to start exercising and eating better. The progress is slower, but the long-term benefits are far greater. Along the way, the discipline and habits you develop make you stronger and more resilient.

Expecting to fix our government by winning one decisive election is the political equivalent of a crash diet. It feels good for a moment—but it always disappoints in the end.

Radical incrementalism, by contrast, takes a different path. Like exercise and healthy eating, the slow and steady approach produces lasting change. It also builds habits, discipline, and resilience—skills that prepare us for future challenges and, over time, deliver transformative results.

This philosophy is deeply rooted in our national heritage. The illegal founding of Harvard University marked the beginning of the colonists' long journey toward self-rule. By creating institutions without the Crown's permission, they learned the practical skills of self-governance. Over the next 140 years, those habits—organizing,

[364] Rauch, *Government's End.*

leading, and governing locally—became the backbone of American independence.

In that same spirit, today's 519,000 state and local officials should be continually seeking ways to move decision-making closer to home. Shifting even a small measure of authority from Washington to a state government—or from a state to a local community—won't change the world overnight. But each small victory weakens the grip of the parasite economy and strengthens the foundations of self-governance.

These officials should also look for opportunities to impose checks and balances on unelected bureaucrats. In theory, Congress should provide that accountability. In practice, it rarely does, because Congress itself is paralyzed. That means the responsibility falls to the states and local governments to find creative workarounds.

One such workaround involves the obscure but powerful tool known as "guidances." Regulators issue guidances to explain how they will interpret or enforce a law. These documents often sound benign—and sometimes they are. But guidances also allow unelected officials to reshape the intent of laws without congressional approval.

Most guidances are sent to state or local agencies, where they are quietly adopted and almost never scrutinized. To restore accountability, every one of the 87,576 state and local governing bodies should require their employees to report all such guidances to their elected officials. Those officials could then decide whether to follow, reject, or challenge them.

Just as shifting authority from the federal level to the states represents progress, adding small checks like these helps reclaim self-governance from the unelected class. Each step, however modest, chips away at the power of the parasite economy and reduces the ability of the Elite One Percent and the Politically Active Elites to impose their will on the American people.

The road ahead is long. But even the longest journey begins with a single step.

Chapter 16

WHO DECIDES?

As America works to end the elitist revolt against its founding ideals, progress will come through both grand and humble moments. There will be inspired campaigns, stirring speeches, and milestones of triumph. There will also be quiet setbacks and unheralded victories that never make the news.

Most of the real work will be slow, steady, and—at times—tedious. That's the essence of radical incrementalism. Sports fans may remember the spectacular catch that wins a Super Bowl, but that moment is made possible only by years of unseen repetition and discipline on practice fields.

Small changes made today can yield profound results a year, a decade, or even a generation from now.

One of the clearest examples comes from 1881, when President James Garfield was shot by a disgruntled job seeker. Tragically, Garfield's greatest misfortune was not the bullet—it was his doctors. Determined to locate and remove the projectile, they ignored emerging medical science.

As Candice Millard recounts in *Destiny of the Republic*, America's top physicians at the time dismissed Dr. Joseph Lister's revolutionary theory of germs and the importance of sterilization. In their frantic effort to find the bullet, a dozen doctors repeatedly probed Garfield's wounds with unwashed hands and unsterilized instruments.[365]

Had they done nothing, Garfield likely would have survived. Instead, he lingered for more than two months before dying—not from the shooting, but from infection. His assassin later remarked, "I shot him, but it was the doctors who killed him."[366]

The tragedy shocked the nation. Newspapers chronicled Garfield's suffering in detail, forcing the public to confront the arrogance and failure of the medical establishment. In its aftermath, American medicine changed course as hospitals and physicians began to embrace Lister's principles of cleanliness. One simple change was to wash hands before treating a patient. This incremental shift in daily practice transformed public health. Within a few decades, life expectancy in the United States rose from the mid-forties to more than sixty.[367]

That's the quiet power of radical incrementalism: small corrections that, over time, save millions of lives.

What lessons does Garfield's story offer for those seeking to restore America's founding ideals? How can it guide state and local leaders working to move decision-making closer to home?

The answer is deceptively simple. America was founded on the belief that governments derive their just powers from the consent of the governed. The Wilsonian elitists reject that belief. They insist that society should be governed by "experts"—people insulated from the voters, convinced that their credentials give them the right to rule.

That is the great divide in American politics today.

---

[365] Candice Millard, *Destiny of the Republic* (Vintage: 2011).

[366] Ibid.

[367] "Annual life expectancy at birth in the United States, from 1850 to 2023, with projections until 2100," Statista, accessed December 12, 2025, https://www.statista.com/statistics/1040079/life-expectancy-united-states-all-time/.

- On one side stands the vast majority of Americans who continue to embrace the founding ideals of freedom, equality, and self-governance.
- On the other stands a small but powerful elite who believe that ordinary citizens are unfit to decide how they will live—that a select few are destined to rule the many.

To defeat the elitist revolt, this contrast must become the centerpiece of our national dialogue. Every debate, every campaign, every conversation should begin with a single, clarifying question:

Who decides?

Once the question is asked, the answer follows naturally. Whenever someone proposes a national solution, ask why it shouldn't be handled by the states. If it's a state issue, ask why it can't be managed locally—or even by families and individuals themselves.

The moment "Who decides?" enters the discussion, those who favor top-down control lose their footing. Most Americans instinctively prefer decisions to be made as close to home as possible. They trust neighbors and local communities far more than unelected officials in Washington.

That is why the question must be asked—and asked again and again.

To be clear, this is not a call for politeness or passivity. Citizens should not meekly attend a meeting, whisper "Who decides?" and return to their seats. They should confront the arrogance of those who believe they have the right to rule over others. The question "What gives you the right?" should ring out with moral conviction—a form of righteous anger grounded in respect for freedom.

But righteous anger must be disciplined. If it erupts into rage, it repels the very Americans whose support we need—the fair-minded citizens, like the two Midwestern women described earlier, who instinctively crave decency and stability. The task, then, is to channel anger into purpose: to act firmly but civilly, to inspire rather than alienate, to remind people who the real adversary is. When we pick our battles carefully and carry ourselves with dignity, the moral contrast between self-governance and rule by elites becomes unmistakable.

Combining righteous anger with disciplined behavior is never easy.

Dr. Martin Luther King Jr. understood this challenge better than anyone. He required every participant in his movement to sign a *Commitment Card*—a personal pledge to uphold the highest standards of conduct.

Commitment Card

Martin Luther King, Jr.
1963

I hereby pledge myself—my person and body—to the nonviolent movement. Therefore I will keep the following ten commandments:

1. Meditate daily on the teachings and life of Jesus.

2. Remember always that the non—violent movement seeks justice and reconciliation — not victory.

3. Walk and talk in the manner of love, for God is love.

4. Pray daily to be used by God in order that all men might be free.

5. Sacrifice personal wishes in order that all men might be free.

6. Observe with both friend and foe the ordinary rules of courtesy.

7. Seek to perform regular service for others and for the world.

8. Refrain from the violence of fist, tongue, or heart.

9. Strive to be in good spiritual and bodily health.

10. Follow the directions of the movement and of the captain on a demonstration.

I sign this pledge, having seriously considered what I do and with the determination and will to persevere.

Name____________________

Address__________________

Phone___________________

Nearest Relative___________

Address__________________

Besides demonstrations, I could also help the movement by (Circle the proper items):
Run errands, Drive my car, Fix food for volunteers, Clerical work, Make phone calls, Answer phones, Mimeograph, Type, Print Signs, Distribute leaflets.

ALABAMA CHRISTIAN MOVEMENT FOR HUMAN RIGHTS
Birmingham Affiliate of S.C.L.C.
505 1/2 North 17th Street
F.L. Shuttlesworth, President

As a Baptist minister, King grounded his campaign in the teachings of Jesus. Yet his "commandments" also offer timeless wisdom for anyone seeking to engage in politics, regardless of faith. His approach reminds us that moral courage, humility, and self-control are the true instruments of lasting change.

Our goal, likewise, is not to vanquish a rival political tribe but to restore America's founding ideals. We want all Americans—left, right, and center—to share in the blessings of freedom, equality, and self-governance.

Cultivating that spirit will take time and discipline. Just as athletes must train before competing for a championship, citizens must prepare before expecting political victory.

A good place to start is by practicing the question that defines self-governance: *Who decides?*

Take any issue you care about and imagine how different the results might be depending on who makes the decision. Then try the same exercise with another issue. Soon, you'll find that almost every public debate—from education to health care to housing—boils down to this one question.

The more you practice, the more naturally you'll be able to explain why decisions made closer to home tend to produce better, fairer, and more durable results.

Consider one simple example.

Should cell phones be banned in classrooms? Polls show that two-thirds of voters say yes. That finding tempts politicians to propose a sweeping national law. But the issue is far from simple. Most parents would rather send their children to a school where phones are allowed, especially if they worry about reaching them in an emergency.[368]

Other complications quickly arise. Should the same rule apply to first graders and high schoolers? To honor students and those who

---

[368] July 16 2025—Napolitan News data from survey of 1,000 registered voters.

struggle? Should bans cover only class time, the entire school day, or just testing periods? If phones are confiscated, who stores them—and what happens when a child needs to contact a parent? Would a total ban discourage at-risk students from attending school at all?

Each of these questions reminds us why local decision-making matters. There is no single right answer for every community in America—and that's precisely the point.

In most political debates today, advocates of a cellphone ban eagerly dive into the details. They debate the pros and cons, weigh competing studies, and search for the elusive "right" answer. The discussion often feels like solving a complex math problem—intricate, technical, and exhausting.

But that's where so many reform efforts go wrong. Once the conversation turns to the technicalities of the "right" policy, it inevitably gets handed over to the "experts." Panels are formed, studies commissioned, and lobbyists activated. Bureaucrats, unions, and advocacy groups swarm in to define what is "best." Before long, the parasite economy is fully engaged—and the outcome reflects the interests of Washington insiders rather than the needs of families.

For those committed to restoring America's founding ideals, the first act of discipline is to resist that trap. We must refuse to start with *what* should be decided and instead begin with *who* should decide. That's not always easy, especially on issues we care about deeply. But without asking the *"Who decides?"* question first, we almost always end up with the wrong answer.

Once that question is asked, everything changes. The debate stops being about the perfect rule and becomes about the rightful decision-maker. Should the policy be set by federal agencies, state legislatures, local school boards—or by parents and teachers themselves?

When voters are asked, their answer is overwhelmingly clear. Only 7 percent say the federal government should decide about cell phones in schools. Just 14 percent say it should be left to state governments. Nearly three out of four—76 percent—want the decision made closer to home.[369]

The lesson is simple but profound: The wisdom of the people is revealed when power is returned to them.

The best solution is the one that gives parents real choices. Let individual schools, or even individual teachers, set their own rules. Allow parents to decide what works for their children. In one community, strict phone bans may be welcomed; in another, flexibility may make more sense. For some parents, the policy might not matter much; for others, it could be essential.

The beauty of self-governance is that it allows both approaches to coexist. Each family, each community, each school should be free to decide for itself—because in America, that's where legitimate authority begins.

This approach offers three powerful benefits of moving decision-making closer to home.

First, it places authority in the hands of those most directly affected. Senior citizens who grew up before the digital revolution may have opinions about smartphones in schools, but the question matters far more to parents of school-aged children.

Second, asking *"Who decides?"* helps reduce conflict. In a national debate over cell phone bans, the two Midwestern women might have differing views and find themselves on opposite political sides. But if each were free to choose what's best for her own family, both could support a solution grounded in choice rather than coercion.

Third, decentralizing decision-making strengthens society's collective wisdom. When communities pursue different approaches, they learn from one another. Parents compare experiences, schools and PTAs exchange lessons, and local leaders refine their policies through observation and adaptation. Over time, this process of

---

369 Ibid.

experimentation builds a vast reservoir of knowledge—a living database of what truly works.

Experience, after all, is the most reliable teacher.

On October 7, 1903, a government-funded effort to build a "flying machine" ended with a crash into the Potomac River. The aircraft, designed by Samuel Langley, secretary of the Smithsonian Institution, had been financed by what was then the largest defense grant in US history. Two days later, *The New York Times* confidently declared that human flight was at least "a million years" away.[370] If someone with Langley's credentials couldn't do it, they reasoned, no one could.

Ironically, that same day the Wright brothers began building their own plane. Nine weeks later, they made history at Kitty Hawk, North Carolina.[371] Lacking formal credentials or government backing, the brothers relied on trial and error, improvisation, and their own homemade wind tunnel. Their success came not from theory but from experimentation—from learning by doing.

That's the essence of self-governance. When decisions are made closer to home, innovation flourishes and knowledge multiplies. Many minds work on the same problems, each contributing insight. The result is not chaos but progress.

Of course, some matters—national defense, Social Security, Medicare—must remain national responsibilities. But those are the exceptions, not the rule. Sixty-one percent of voters think nearly everything else can be decided closer to home—by states, communities, families, and individuals.[372]

Years ago, I opened a speech at the Heritage Foundation by declaring that nobody in America cares about limited government.

---

370 NY Times, *Flying Machines Which Do Not Fly*, Oct 9, 1903.

371 David McCullough, *The Wright Brothers* (Simon & Schuster: 2016).

372 June 30–July 1, 2025—Napolitan News data from survey of 1,000 registered voters.

That line startled the audience. After all, a commitment to limited government is literally etched into the walls of the Heritage building. Their entire mission was built around that idea.

I quickly explained that voters don't care about limited government—or big government, or any particular kind of government. Most Americans rarely think about government at all. What they do care deeply about is the society they live in. They care about the world their children are growing up in, and they long for a place where people can live freely according to their own values.

What people are hungering for is not a government that works—it's a society that works. That's why I urged the audience to stop talking about *limited government* and start talking about the kind of society that limited government would create.

The same logic applies to those of us working to restore a self-governing society by bringing decision-making closer to home. We must do our homework—and we must be able to paint a picture of what that looks like in the lives of ordinary Americans. When it comes to cell phones in classrooms, for example, it's not about political theory. It's about what's best for the children.

The image we paint will often reveal the same three great benefits of bottom-up decision-making: It empowers those most affected by an issue, reduces unnecessary conflict, and expands our shared knowledge. But those benefits are a means, not an end. Our goal isn't to win an argument about government structure—it's to show how self-governance can build a society that actually works.

In 1881, doctors began washing their hands before treating patients. They knew it helped, but few could have imagined how dramatically that simple habit would increase life expectancy in America.

Today, those who want to restore America's founding ideals must adopt a similarly modest but transformative habit. We should begin every political discussion by asking one simple question: Who decides?

If that question became as natural as washing our hands before dinner, it would revolutionize our political culture and renew the health of American self-governance for generations to come.

And there is no one better positioned to lead that renewal than the nation's 519,000 state and local elected officials. In their hands, the messenger becomes the message—and the restoration of a self-governing society begins anew.

Chapter 17

AN ACTION PLAN

To defeat the elitist revolt and restore America's founding ideals, the nation's 519,000 state and local elected officials must fulfill the role James Madison envisioned when he wrote that "Ambition must be made to counteract ambition."[373]

That doesn't mean pretending that local officials are saints and national leaders are sinners. They're all human. In 1755, George Washington lost a race for the Virginia House of Burgesses because his opponent offered voters free alcohol. Three years later, Washington followed suit—providing beer, wine, brandy, and rum punch to secure his first electoral victory.[374]

Most local officials today are genuinely motivated by public service. But in any group that large, there will be scoundrels and opportunists. Not only that, some enter office with one eye already on Washington, intent not on governing locally but on climbing the political ladder.

We don't need perfection. We need public servants who love their country, care about their communities, and understand that decision-making should move closer to the people. Every transfer

---

[373] Madison and Hamilton, "Federalist 51."

[374] Dennis J. Pogue, *Founding Spirits* (Harbour Books: 2011).

of power—from the federal government to the states, and from the states to localities—is a victory for self-governance.

To play their part in that process, state and local leaders must adopt new habits—political routines that begin every debate with the question, "Who decides?" Officials animated by righteous anger toward those who presume to rule over others will find purpose in this discipline. The routines themselves will cultivate the steadiness needed to communicate the message persuasively—to those same fair-minded Americans represented by the two Midwestern women.

There is no magic formula for this work. Renewal depends on the daily practice of healthy political habits. Sometimes that may mean adding "Who should decide?" as the first item on a city council agenda. Other times it may mean creating a recurring agenda line devoted to identifying and challenging specific examples of federal overreach.

The key is persistence: asking the question again and again until it becomes second nature—until self-governance feels less like a slogan and more like a civic reflex.

Earlier, I mentioned how federal regulators routinely issue "guidances" to state and local governments. While some are helpful, the process is often abused. Regulators use it to reinterpret laws and advance their own agendas—quietly expanding federal authority without congressional approval.

In most communities today, local bureaucrats decide whether to follow Washington's "guidance." But imagine how different the process would be if all 87,586 state and local governing bodies adopted a simple "hand-washing" exercise—beginning each meeting with a review of every relevant federal guidance.

In some cases, the outcome would be merely comic, exposing the absurdity of our top-down Wilsonian system. One Department of Transportation guidance, for example, discouraged using pop-culture references or humor on changeable road signs—warning that it might "adversely affect respect for the sign."[375]

Yet many state and local agencies have found that humor works. Drivers in Texas or Indiana might respond well to clever or light-hearted messages that Washington bureaucrats might not understand. Maybe federal officials simply lack a sense of humor, or maybe they consider road signs too solemn for levity. Either way, there's no reason a distant bureaucrat should decide whether local officials can post a joke about seatbelts.

Of course, the fate of the republic doesn't hinge on roadside wit. But the practice of reviewing federal guidances could become a powerful tool for addressing far more consequential matters—immigration policy, hiring practices, gender-identity rules, racial-discrimination claims, and environmental regulations among them.

Those decisions should rest with local elected officials, and the review process itself should become as routine as washing hands before dinner. Most guidances would likely be accepted, but not all. Some would be rejected. Others would be sent back for clarification.

The immediate impact of rejecting a federal guidance would usually be modest but meaningful. It would reaffirm that local standards are set by accountable representatives, not unelected officials in a distant capital. In most cases, the rejection wouldn't even trigger a federal response.

Still, each act of defiance—each school board, town council, or county commission questioning or rejecting a Washington directive—would make news. And if many local governments began pushing back together, Washington would have no choice but to notice.

If each of America's 87,586 state and local governing bodies rejected even one federal guidance per month, Washington bureaucrats would face more than a million rejections every year. Each

---

[375] SPN Center for Practical Federalism. https://www.centerforpracticalfederalism.org/

rejection would generate new headaches—tough questions from Congress, unflattering press coverage, and growing public skepticism toward the regulatory machine.

This matters because repetition works. The average person must hear something seven times before it sinks in. If federal regulators were asked a million times a year why anyone should follow their "guidance," the message would begin to land. Faced with persistent scrutiny from below, regulators might even grow more cautious about issuing unnecessary directives.

In an ideal world, state and local elected officials would ask the *"Who decides?"* question as naturally as doctors wash their hands before treating a patient. And with nearly a thousand local officials for every member of Congress, that message could echo day after day, meeting after meeting, issue after issue—until the entire parasite economy began to have nightmares about it.

But long-term success will require more than new agenda items or routine pushback. State and local officials must also take initiative—driving policy debates and advancing ideas that shift power toward the people.

A vivid example is the movement to give parents greater control over where their children go to school. In recent years, a growing number of states have adopted laws allowing education funding to follow the student. The results have been remarkable: Millions of families now enjoy greater choice and flexibility, and local communities are rethinking the purpose of public education itself.

That's the model for future reform. State and local leaders should constantly look for creative ways to strengthen society by moving decision-making closer to home.

Of course, this decentralized approach will sometimes yield quirky laws. New Jersey, for instance, remains the only state that bans self-service gas stations—a rule memorialized in T-shirts declaring, "Jersey Girls Don't Pump Gas." Having lived there myself, I found the ban mildly annoying but also endearing—a peculiar local custom that gave the state character. It certainly didn't require federal intervention.

More importantly, local creativity can sometimes produce innovations that challenge federal authority in bold and consequential ways.

One of the most promising opportunities for reform lies in the culture wars surrounding higher education. Many state leaders find it absurd that federal bureaucrats and newly elected presidents can rewrite the rules for colleges every four years. They would rather see universities governed by policies that reflect their own state's values and protected from the ideological whiplash of national politics.

The challenge is that the only way to insulate a state's colleges from federal control is to free them from dependence on Washington's student-loan programs. Those loans are so deeply embedded in the system that it's almost impossible to imagine higher education without them.

One simple but perilous approach would be for a state to ban its colleges from accepting federal student loans altogether. That would make it nearly impossible for those schools to attract students. Solving that problem would require creative thought and strategies—like those that got women the vote and ended legalized racism in Montgomery.

There's no off-the-shelf solution for a governor to "plug and play."

Still, an innovative leader could explore several paths. One option would be to create a state-run student-loan program to replace the federal plan entirely. For students and schools, little would change—except that colleges would no longer be subject to the policy whims of each new administration.

Another possibility would be to revive the pre-federal model and form partnerships with private lenders. Whether through a state program or a public-private system, parents and students alike would celebrate the day they never had to fill out another FAFSA form.

Other models could also emerge. Some states are already offering free tuition for low-income students. Others could require wealthy universities with large endowments to fund their own student-loan programs. Private colleges might be given incentives to reject federal funds altogether.

Visionary leaders pursue such ideas not because they are easy, but because their long-term impact can be transformative. It took twenty-two years to go from the first meeting of colonial leaders at the Stamp Act Congress to the ratification of the US Constitution. It took fifty years from Wyoming's first suffrage law to the Nineteenth Amendment. And it took seventeen years from Jackie Robinson's Major League debut to the passage of the Civil Rights Act.

Every great transformation begins with a single step. The one we ask local and state officials to take is to keep asking, day after day, *"Who decides?"*

Perhaps the greatest opportunity for transformational change lies in healthcare. In a well-functioning system, patients and their families would make important medical decisions in consultation with doctors they know and trust. Today, however, those decisions are largely dictated by unelected government officials and insurance-company bureaucrats.

Roughly half of all healthcare spending now comes directly from the federal government. On top of that, federal rules tightly control the insurance employers must provide and the plans available through Obamacare exchanges. Meanwhile, a wave of consolidation has allowed giant healthcare corporations to swallow competitors and grow increasingly detached from patients.

While exact numbers are hard to pin down, most Americans control only about 10 to 15 percent of their own healthcare spending. On the "Who decides?" scale, America's healthcare system earns a failing grade.

If we could change the system so that consumers controlled 35, 40, or even 50 percent of healthcare decision-making, the system would look—and function—very differently. It would respond to the needs of patients, not the whining of bureaucrats.

The good news is that voters see the problem. Sixty-four percent believe that individuals and their doctors—not government regulators or insurance companies—should have the most control over healthcare decisions. Only one in four think more regulation is the answer.[376]

As with higher education, it's easy to imagine potential solutions but harder to implement them. One practical reform would be to let people buy any insurance product approved by their state insurance commissioner. Polling consistently shows that a strong majority of voters support this idea.

Why does it matter? Because healthcare needs and community values in Idaho are not the same as in New York. An insurance commissioner in Idaho would likely approve more flexible, affordable plans than one in New York. Idaho voters would gain more control over their healthcare choices, and the nation could see firsthand whether localized decision-making leads to better results.

Unfortunately, states currently lack the authority to pursue such reforms without federal approval. Any state that wanted to experiment would have to design its own plan and apply for a federal waiver. The effort would demand time, persistence, and political will—but the potential benefits would be immense.

Another promising idea would be to require employers to offer the coverage currently mandated by Obamacare while giving workers the option to opt out and keep the savings. In other words, if an employee didn't want every benefit included in a standard plan, they could choose less expensive coverage and receive the cost difference as additional pay. Polling suggests 83 percent of voters support this

376 Dec 17–18, 2024—Napolitan News data from survey of 1,000 registered voters.

idea.[377] Once again, it would give individuals—not bureaucracies—more control over their own choices.

Of course, such reforms would face fierce resistance from insurance companies, major healthcare corporations, and the full force of the parasite economy. Their opposition would be driven by the same motive that led liquor companies to oppose women's suffrage: It would cut into profits.

Meanwhile, the hyper-partisan federal establishment remains determined to keep control in Washington—if only to fight over who gets to make the rules. When one side wins, the rules are written by Dr. Anthony Fauci; when the other wins, by HHS Secretary Robert F. Kennedy. In their world, control over healthcare policy is simply another prize of political victory.

That's precisely why America needs state and local leaders willing to act creatively and persistently to move power back to the people. Protecting colleges from Washington's culture wars will take time. Empowering citizens to control their own healthcare will take even longer.

Progress may come slowly, sometimes advancing two steps forward and one step back. But every great movement for freedom began the same way—with a disciplined commitment to ask, before every decision, "*Who decides?*"

The moment that question becomes instinctive for citizens and leaders alike, the elitist revolt will finally meet its match.

---

377 Oct 15–16, 2025—Napolitan News data from survey of 1,000 registered voters.

Chapter 18

MAKING THE IMPOSSIBLE SEEM INEVITABLE

From the vantage point of the twenty-first century, America's founding can appear inevitable—almost natural. In the century and a half between the Puritans' landing at Plymouth Rock and the War for Independence, the American colonies developed a culture that was both rooted in and distinct from England's.

Part of that new culture grew from small acts of self-determination—like founding Harvard College without asking the king's permission. The colonists didn't realize it at the time, but that pragmatic step helped lay the foundation for a self-governing society.

The emergence of a uniquely colonial culture did not go unnoticed in London. Benjamin Franklin envisioned an empire on both sides of the Atlantic and predicted that one day, "the greatest number of Englishmen would be on this side of the water."[378] But historian Kevin Phillips observed that it wasn't long before "British politicians started talking about not letting the American colonies spread out

---

[378] Kevin Phillips, *1775: A Good Year for Revolution* (Penguin Random House: 2013).

or get too big."[379] As the two cultures drifted further apart, each side came to see the other as exploitative.

Tensions made conflict inevitable—but the Revolution itself was not preordained. It was shaped by the individual decisions of ordinary colonists.

It was shaped by Paul Revere's midnight ride and by the seventy "Minute Men" who answered his call in Lexington. At dawn on April 19, 1775, they faced British regulars. Eight were killed in the brief skirmish, a sacrifice that turned the "shot heard 'round the world" into a defining moment of history.

That first battle inspired others to join the fight. By year's end, "a few square miles of Boston represented the sole remaining seat of British occupation" in the colonies.[380]

It was also shaped by a web of self-created institutions that began governing the colonies long before independence was declared. Hundreds of local committees and colonial assemblies "began to exercise power twelve to eighteen months before" the Declaration of Independence.[381] In effect, British rule had already been replaced by de facto American self-rule.

When all was said and done, the emergence of a distinctly colonial culture made conflict unavoidable—but the Revolution itself was carried out by countless colonists whose names have been lost to history. As John Adams later reflected, "The Revolution was effected before the war commenced. The Revolution was in the minds and hearts of the people."[382]

To understand our own moment in history, it helps to remember that the past never felt inevitable to those who lived it. The

---

[379] Ibid.

[380] Ibid.

[381] Ibid.

[382] John Adams, letter from John Adams to Hezekiah Niles, archives at Founders Online, February 13, 1818, https://founders.archives.gov/documents/Adams/99-02-02-6854.

men we honor as Founding Fathers were once branded as traitors by King George. Had the Revolution failed, they likely would have been executed.

Even earlier, the colonists who founded Harvard in 1636 had no idea they were laying the groundwork for an unprecedented experiment in self-governance. They simply wanted to create a college free from royal interference in theology. The same was true of countless other settlers who followed their example, forming churches, towns, and associations without asking permission from anyone.

In doing so, they created a new social order without intending to—or even realizing it.

The process resembled raising children: Parents are too busy nurturing and adapting to notice how much their children have changed. Then one day, at a family reunion, relatives who haven't seen the kids in years are stunned by how much they've grown.

So it was with the colonists. As their culture drifted from that of the mother country, few noticed the magnitude of the change. Even as late as 1776, most still thought of themselves as loyal British subjects. They didn't set out to launch a new political order; they were simply trying to build better lives for their families and neighbors.

Why does this matter?

Because twenty-first-century Americans are living through a remarkably similar transformation.

Just as the colonists unwittingly built a new social order, we have been creating a decentralized one. The digital revolution has completely transformed how we live, work, and relate to one another. It happened so gradually that we hardly noticed. Like watching a niece or nephew grow up, the full scale of change only becomes clear in hindsight.

Not long ago, there was just a single college football game on television each weekend, and few professional sports were broadcast at all. Today, no one could possibly watch every game played in a single day. We've gone from marveling at the convenience of ATMs to rarely using cash; from treasuring a handwritten letter that arrived once a week to assuming we've been ghosted if a text goes unanswered for an hour.

Now, with smartphones, wearable devices, and near-constant connectivity, the pace of change has only accelerated. My watch congratulates me for getting a good night's sleep and counts my steps, while artificial intelligence ushers in an even deeper transformation—one that could rival or surpass the Industrial Revolution in scope and speed.

These shifts have wiped out entire industries, created new ones, and fundamentally altered how Americans work, play, socialize, and learn. They have also produced a cultural divide between the American people and the Wilsonian elitists that rivals the gulf between colonial Americans and King George.

Like King George long ago, the Wilsonian elitists never saw it coming. As Steve Jobs and Bill Gates launched the digital revolution by founding Apple and Microsoft, President Jimmy Carter's *National Agenda for the '80s* didn't even mention the word "computer." That omission captured how little the ruling class understood the transformation already underway—and how poorly they still grasp its implications.

In this new environment, the bureaucratic, top-down government that ruled America in the 1960s and '70s is no more suited to our decentralized society than the British monarchy was to colonial America.

The tension between a centralizing government and a decentralizing people means that twenty-first-century political conflict is inevitable. But the outcome is not. It will be shaped by millions of individual choices—and by the collective wisdom, courage, and perseverance of the American people in the years ahead.

To understand how individuals can help move the nation forward, we must first understand the political environment. Three numbers define it: 80, 1, and 519,000.

The first number, 80, represents the 80 percent—the vast majority of Americans who don't live and breathe politics but who still embrace the nation's founding ideals. They agree with the timeless belief that all people are "endowed by their Creator with certain unalienable Rights," and that governments derive their just powers from "the consent of the governed."[383]

The 80 percent includes people like the two Midwestern women who thought they were political opposites. It includes even some of the angriest voters. Their focus is not on the size or role of government but on the kind of society they want to live in.

They want a society that works rather than a government that works. They want people to come together and build stronger communities. They long for a system that restores power to voters rather than bureaucrats.

The 80 percent want the freedom to live their own lives and to pursue a dizzying variety of passions, beliefs, and lifestyles. That is what you would expect from a people who believe that everyone should be free to live as they choose—so long as their choices don't infringe on the rights of others to do the same.

Despite what we hear from Washington and the national media, most Americans are not hopelessly divided. The riddle of partisan polarization is largely an illusion—one sustained by elites and institutions that profit from anger and conflict. The more the elites can convince citizens that their neighbors are the enemy, the less everyday Americans will recognize how much common ground they actually share.

---

383 June 26, 2023—Napolitan News data from survey of 1,000 registered voters.

The last thing the elites want us to recognize is that the 80 percent are the reason to be optimistic about America's future. They remain, as Lincoln said of the Union itself, "the last best hope of earth."[384]

The second number, 1, refers to the Elite One Percent—an extraordinarily powerful class whose views are increasingly disconnected from those of the American public. Not all elites are elitists, but this group is dominated by those who reject America's founding ideals and who are indifferent to the will of voters. At the most basic level, most Americans want decisions made closer to home. The elitists want the opposite.

Making matters worse, as political scientist Aaron Wildavsky noted long ago, many elitists want to purge society "of the values, tastes, preferences, and policies desired by the mass of Americans."[385] They seek to use the power of government to reshape American life according to their own utopian vision—a vision most Americans find deeply alien and offensive.

Over the past four decades, this elitist revolt has pushed the federal government further from both the American people and from the nation's founding ideals. It also created the parasite economy, which serves elites and the politically well-connected rather than everyday Americans. That bias was exposed during the 2008–09 financial crisis, when government efforts focused on rescuing big banks and Wall Street instead of Main Street.

A government run by elites, for bureaucrats, and for whatever they decide is "best for the people" has fueled deep anger and frustration among ordinary Americans. The first stirrings of revolt took shape when President George H. W. Bush broke his "no new taxes" pledge and fractured the Reagan coalition. What followed was a

---

[384] Abraham Lincoln, transcript of "Second Annual Message," archived at Miller Center, University of Virginia, December 1, 1862, https://millercenter.org/the-presidency/presidential-speeches/december-1-1862-second-annual-message.

[385] Wildavsky, *Revolt.*

string of ten consecutive close presidential elections, culminating in the election of Donald Trump in 2016 and 2024.

The anger of voters had been building for decades as government elitists ignored them. Today, however, it is the anger of the Wilsonian elitists that drives the political narrative. They are offended by the fact that 82 percent of Americans believe "graduating from a top university does not make someone better qualified to govern."[386] Like the Harvard professor who once complained that voters expected to be heard, many elites are enraged that voters refuse to stay silent and simply let the elitists rule.

Over the past decade, the political landscape has shifted again. In President Trump's second term, the battle no longer pits a distant ruling class against frustrated citizens. Instead, two political armies now fight for dominance within the Capitol itself. Both claim to speak for the American people, and both seek to wield government power to impose their preferred vision on the nation. Yet neither side is interested in returning power to the voters.

President Trump's rebellion against the political establishment was both genuine and revealing. Like *The Hunger Games* rebels of District 13, his movement exposed the corruption of the ruling class but still fought on the same terrain. His presidency broke the illusion of elite competence and proved that the system could be challenged. Yet it also showed how difficult it is to restore a self-governing society using the very instruments of centralized power.

Voters recognize the problem. Seventy percent believe senior leaders of federal agencies pursue their own agendas rather than carry out the will of the people.[387] That frustration helps explain why 81 percent of voters favor term limits for federal agency leaders.[388]

---

[386] December 26-29, 2025, YouGov data from survey of 1,550 U.S. adult citizens.

[387] June 17–18, 2024—Napolitan News data from survey of 1,000 registered voters.

[388] August 13–14—Napolitan News data from survey of 1,000 registered voters.

This dynamic presents a simple but profound choice for the nation. Do we want a government that serves the Elite One Percent—or a self-governing society that serves the 80 percent and puts voters back in charge?

Do we want whichever political army won the last election to rewrite the rules of society, only to have those rules overturned in the next election? Or do we want to empower everyday Americans to make the important decisions about their own lives?

The answers are obvious to nearly everyone except a handful of elitists. Still, getting from where we are today to a genuinely self-governing society will not be easy. We must never underestimate the lengths to which elitists will go to protect their power.

When the Wright brothers embarrassed the Smithsonian Institution, the backlash was intense. A plane developed by Smithsonian Secretary Samuel Langley had crashed spectacularly just months before the Wright brothers' first successful flight. Yet the Smithsonian refused to acknowledge what the brothers had achieved. For years, the museum brazenly displayed Langley's failed aircraft as the "first man-carrying aeroplane in the history of the world capable of sustained flight."[389]

It's almost unbelievable. The nation's most prestigious museum knowingly displayed a plane that had failed—and falsely claimed it was the first to fly. That episode could fairly be called an early case of disinformation.

It took decades before the Smithsonian finally acknowledged the truth. The *Wright Flyer* was not placed on display in that museum until forty-five years after its historic flight. In fact, the Smithsonian waited until eleven months after Orville Wright passed away before finally displaying the plane (Wilbur had died much earlier). The embarrassment of the Smithsonian prevented the Wright brothers from being officially acknowledged during their lifetime.

---

[389] McCullough, *The Wright Brothers.*

The same sort of resistance can be expected from any effort that takes power, money, or prestige away from the Wilsonian government of the unelected.

That's where the third number comes in—the nation's 519,000 state and local elected officials. These officials reflect the views of everyday Americans more authentically than anyone in official Washington ever could. They are best positioned to push back against the parasite economy and the Wilsonian system of government.

In practical terms, the most important way these officials can represent the 80 percent is by asking a simple question at the start of every meeting and political discussion: *"Who decides?"* Once that question is raised, the Elite One Percent are put on the defensive. The answer, in most cases, will be that decisions should be made locally—or by individuals. From there, the challenge is simply finding creative ways to make it happen.

These state and local elected officials also play a crucial role in giving everyday Americans a voice. Members of Congress may find it easy to ignore voters, but local officials are not so distant. Voters can find them at the grocery store, the ballfield, or the July Fourth picnic. Their closeness to the community—and their ability to be heard in the halls of power—make them an essential conduit in the national political dialogue.

In short, the Elite One Percent are the problem. The 80 percent are the solution. And the 519,000 are the means through which the 80 percent can restore America's founding ideals.

The good news is that we are riding the wave of a decentralizing society. Every day, new technologies make it harder for top-down government to survive. The Elite One Percent and their media gatekeepers can no longer control the national agenda or silence inconvenient voices.

But victory for the 80 percent is not automatic. Restoring a self-governing society will require effort and sacrifice from countless ordinary citizens. It will require leaders who understand that trust in government cannot be demanded—it must be earned by listening to voters and respecting their freedoms.

To defeat the elitist revolt, we must always stay focused on who the real enemy is—the Wilsonian elitists and the corrupt system of government by the unelected that empowers them. In *The Hunger Games* imagery, the real enemy is both the forces of the Capitol and the forces of District 13. In America today, it is both the descendants of the New Left and the opposing elitists who arose to fight the New Left. Both want to remake American society in their own utopian image.

To be clear, not even all of the "ten-percenters" who engage in daily political battles embrace the un-American views of the Wilsonian elitists. Many are simply engaged because they enjoy politics and policy. Some feel strongly that one political team is better for the country, while others see their engagement as a form of damage control. Still, it's important to remember that many of these activists would welcome a system in which voters are truly in charge.

Once you realize how small a segment of the population the real enemy represents, it becomes clear that both Midwestern women are potential allies. They may disagree on a few policies, but their shared values and history bind them to a belief in America's founding ideals. They feel as though they're on opposite sides of a political battlefield only because the real enemy has pitted them against each other. And they both reject the idea that some people are destined to rule over them.

In addition to remembering who the real enemy is, we must also remember what it is we are fighting for.

Americans today often struggle to recall how different life was in the 1960s and '70s. It is even harder to remember what life was like before the founding of our nation. For more than two thousand years, philosophers, scholars, and kings mocked the idea that people could govern themselves. The founding and success of America proved them wrong.

If we fail to defeat the elitist revolt and restore America's founding ideals, it may be a very long time before the world sees those noble principles rise again.

Victory may seem impossible today because the path forward is difficult to see clearly. The elitists have the vast power of government on their side. But we have something stronger. The American people still believe in the enduring ideals of freedom, equality, and self-governance.

I don't know exactly what the path will look like, but I remain confident that America's best days are still to come. However unpredictable the journey, future historians will likely describe it as inevitable—just as the founding of our free and self-governing nation now seems inevitable to us.

As it was in 1776, so it is today: the fate of freedom depends not on the powerful few but on the countless citizens who still believe in America's promise.

Chapter 19

RENEWING THE AMERICAN PROMISE

As America approaches its 250th birthday, we have much to be thankful for. We are blessed to live in a land founded on the noble ideals of freedom, equality, and self-governance. Those principles remain the foundation of our national identity. As heirs to this remarkable legacy, we bear a solemn responsibility to preserve it—and to pass it on stronger than we found it.

Yet throughout our history, there have always been some who rejected those ideals and believed that a select few were destined to rule the rest. They echo Woodrow Wilson's complaint that the American people never truly "got over" the Declaration of Independence. Like Wilson, today's elitists believe voters are too ignorant—or too unruly—to be trusted with power.

They are wrong. America's greatness has never come from the wisdom of rulers, but from the courage and creativity of free people. Ours is an exceptional nation precisely because of the truths articulated in the Declaration of Independence. When citizens are free to pursue their dreams—to build, to innovate, to fail and try again—extraordinary things happen.

Still, the elitists never give up. Their struggle against self-governance is as old as the republic itself. Once again, we twenty-first-century Americans find ourselves engaged in what Abraham Lincoln called "a great test." Our actions in the years ahead will determine whether a nation "conceived in liberty, and dedicated to the proposition that all men are created equal...can long endure."[390]

To defeat the elitist revolt, Americans must once again rise to meet the challenge John F. Kennedy issued more than sixty years ago: "Ask not what your country can do for you—ask what you can do for your country."[391]

In 1961, that line was widely understood as a call to public service, inspiring thousands to join the Peace Corps and other government programs. At the time, that interpretation made sense. The Wilsonian model of centralized, top-down government was still at its zenith, and faith in large institutions was near its peak.

Today, the context is profoundly different. In the twenty-first century, the most important thing Americans can do for their country is not serving in a government program—it's helping to rebuild a self-governing society grounded in the nation's founding ideals.

What can each of us do to make that happen?

On one level, there is no single answer. The opportunities to strengthen self-governance will vary from place to place and person to person. But history shows that small actions, taken by determined individuals, can transform a nation.

Consider education. Until the mid-twentieth century, school choice was a natural part of American life. As late as the 1940s, most teenagers didn't attend high school at all; families could choose

---

390 Lincoln, "Gettysburg Address."

391 John F. Kennedy, "Inaugural Address," archived at National Archives, January 20, 1961, https://www.archives.gov/milestone-documents/president-john-f-kennedys-inaugural-address.

between work and continued schooling.[392] That freedom narrowed as compulsory education expanded. By the 1950s, more than 90 percent of teenagers were enrolled in high school—and for the first time, federal and state governments began shaping the formative years of nearly every young American.[393]

Recognizing the risks of ceding so much influence to unelected bureaucrats, economist Milton Friedman sounded the alarm. His 1955 essay "The Role of Government in Education" laid the intellectual foundation for today's school-choice movement—a reminder that big changes often begin as small, unpopular ideas advanced by courageous individuals.[394]

Why did it take so long for Friedman's idea to gain traction?

Part of the reason is that, in the 1950s and '60s, most Americans still trusted the federal government. Parents couldn't yet see what Friedman knew—that centralized education would eventually erode local control. Additionally, the national focus at the time was elsewhere. The major education debate of that era centered on racial integration. In 1971, the Supreme Court ruled that it was constitutional to bus students across district lines to achieve racial balance, a policy that dominated headlines and divided communities for more than a decade.[395]

Still, Friedman never stopped pressing his case. His ideas found new audiences during the Reagan years, but they remained on the margins. The real breakthrough came half a century later, during the COVID-19 pandemic. When public schools shut down for months,

---

[392] Thomas D. Snyder, ed., "120 Years of American Education: A Statistical Portrait," National Center for Education Statistics, https://nces.ed.gov/pubs93/93442.pdf.

[393] Ibid.

[394] Milton Friedman, "The Role of Government in Education," 1955 (accessed December 12, 2025), https://la.utexas.edu/users/hcleaver/330T/350kPEEFriedmanRoleOfGovttable.pdf.

[395] Swann v. Charlotte-Mecklenburg Board of Education, 402 US 1 (1971).

parents finally saw what their children were being taught—and how little say they had in the process. That experience awakened a powerful desire to reclaim control. Many discovered that private and charter schools taught more academic skills and less ideological indoctrination. Not only that, but they also reopened far sooner, offering a stark contrast to the inertia of the public system.

Sixty-five years after Friedman first asked *"Who decides?"* about the education of America's children, the opportunity arrived—and change followed almost overnight. The school-choice movement advanced rapidly because its advocates framed the issue around that timeless question. It wasn't about ideology or education theory. It was about power: Who decides what children learn—the government or their parents?

That's the model for all of us to follow.

What Americans can do for their country today is to make *"Who decides?"* the central question in every political discussion. As noted earlier, it should become second nature for state and local leaders—and for ordinary citizens—to ask it whenever new policies are proposed.

Fortunately, most of the reforms needed to restore a self-governing society won't take seventy years to succeed. The tide has already turned. Friedman was writing at a time when American society was still centralizing, and government expansion rode that same wave. Today, we're the ones riding the wave. Our wave is a decentralizing society, one that gives natural momentum to efforts that return decisions to families, communities, and voters themselves. The more often we raise the question *"Who decides?"* the more that momentum will grow.

If you raise this question consistently—in any setting—you will inevitably encounter elitists who reject America's founding ideals and recoil at the idea that voters should be in charge. Some may even say it outright: They believe that voters are stupid.

The natural impulse in that moment is to push back, to argue, to prove them wrong. All of us have been there. We get so focused on winning the argument that we forget the larger point. When our opponent says something insulting or condescending, it's easy to lose our focus and respond in kind.

That's usually a mistake. I learned that lesson long ago during the term-limits movement.

Decades ago, our polling found that nearly 75 percent of voters supported term limits for members of Congress. That wasn't surprising. But we wanted to see what would happen if voters heard the arguments against them. Could anything persuade the public that term limits were a bad idea?

We tested several of those arguments. One of the most common insider complaints was that term limits would force out veteran lawmakers with a lot of experience. The results were remarkable. After hearing arguments against term limits, public support actually increased. What insiders saw as a problem, voters saw as a bonus—another reason to back reform.

That experience led us to a simple conclusion: There was no need to debate point by point. Why refute an argument that only strengthens your case? Instead, we encouraged our allies to stay focused on the positive case for term limits and the broader message of restoring accountability.

The same lesson applies today. When you raise the question "Who decides?" do it with quiet confidence. The American people already agree with you. If someone mocks or dismisses the idea of returning decision-making power to families and communities, let them talk. They're making your argument for you.

At the same time, we should keep sharing a positive message about bringing decisions closer to the people they affect. We don't need to win a debate in the court of public opinion—we've already won "the minds and hearts of the people." The vast majority of Americans are on our side.

If we communicate this message clearly and calmly, we remind people of a simple truth: The Wilsonian elitists are the problem, the 80 percent are the solution, and we stand with the 80 percent. Once we've established that trust, we can show how the nation's 519,000 state and local officials are the means through which the 80 percent can restore America's founding ideals.

We should never tire of repeating this good news. A bottom-up approach to governance empowers those most affected by decisions, reduces political conflict, and expands the pool of knowledge that a free society draws upon.

Despite the ongoing threat from the Wilsonian elitists and the warring political armies in Washington, I remain convinced that America's best days lie ahead. The 250th birthday of our nation offers a chance not merely to celebrate our history, but to renew our promise. We are well positioned to win the battle for America's future because the American people still believe in the ideals of freedom, equality, and self-governance. Just as important, the 519,000 men and women serving in local and state elected offices continue to provide the backbone of a self-governing society.

If we want to make this bright future real for our children and grandchildren, the most important thing we can do for our country is to make *"Who decides?"* the first question in every political conversation. For all Americans, that question should become as natural as washing our hands before dinner.

By doing so, we will have done our part to ensure that "government of the people, by the people, and for the people shall not perish from the earth."

Acknowledgments

This book is the result of decades spent studying public opinion and America's political system. When I conducted my first poll back in the 1980s, I had no idea where the journey would take me—or that the nation was about to embark on an unprecedented string of close presidential elections.

I am deeply grateful to Al Regnery for his encouragement to write this book and for his patience as I missed deadlines along the way. I also appreciate his pairing me with Daniel Allott as my editor. Nobody enjoys having their work critiqued line by line, but I have to admit that Daniel made the final product much, much stronger. On top of that, it was a pleasure working with him.

Eric O'Keefe is a friend I've known since the 1980s. We worked closely together in the term-limits movement and on many other projects over the years. I am grateful for the untold hours he spent reviewing every page—sometimes through several revisions. As he has done throughout our friendship, Eric consistently offered invaluable insights that improved the final product.

My wife, Laura, deserves a special award for enduring the time it took to write and finish this book. More importantly, she is my front-line editor for everything I publish. Before any draft ever reached Daniel or Eric, Laura made it presentable and coherent.

I have also been blessed with two sons who don't mind challenging their father and helping me see things more clearly. Over the years, their questions and debates have been invaluable in helping me look at issues from different perspectives.

Leslie Graves, the CEO of Ballotpedia and perhaps the wisest woman in the political world, kept pushing me to recognize the importance of the 519,000 state and local elected officials.

A special shout-out goes to the two Midwestern women. In reality, they are a composite of four Midwestern women I've known for longer than any of us would like to admit. However, to preserve those friendships, I will refrain from disclosing their names.

Todd and Amy Marshall also took the time to give helpful feedback on the early chapters.

Julie Tisdale, an RMG employee, kept finding the polling numbers I needed and made sure I reported them accurately. Kiernan Tollefson and Chad DeSota also played key roles in generating the research needed for this book and for our other projects.

Going back even further, Howie Rich was the driving force behind the term-limits movement. He was also my first polling client—and remains a client today. Without Howie, I never would have started down this path.

Sid Milkis, now at the University of Virginia, was an important part of my education at DePauw University. He helped me place contemporary politics within the larger sweep of American history.

The late Mary Lou Brewer was my twelfth-grade history teacher. When I entered her class, I hated history (and school). When I left, I was poised to become a history major, and the study of history became a lifelong passion.

In the polling field, I've already mentioned how gracious Joe Napolitan was to give his time to a high school student who didn't even know what to ask. Barry Sussman of *The Washington Post* also took time early in my career to help me express polling data more clearly.

I spent many hours learning from and debating with the late Pat Caddell, one of the best pollsters and analysts of our time. I dearly wish he were still here to help refine some of the ideas in this book.

I also had the pleasure of working with—and writing a book with—pollster Doug Schoen.

All these experiences, and countless others, helped shape my polling career and the themes explored in this book.

Finally, I'd like to thank my agents, Scott Miller and Drew Young of the Gray Miller Agency.

About the Author

Scott Rasmussen has long been recognized as one of the world's leading public opinion pollsters and top political analysts. He is the president of RMG Research and founder of the Napolitan Institute.

Innovation has been a hallmark of Scott's career. In 1978 he changed the world of sports as cofounder of ESPN, taking advantage of the then new technology of satellite communications. As the internet came to life in the '90s, Scott became the first pollster to offer data directly to the public rather than through a network reporter. Scott later revolutionized the polling industry with automated polling, being described by *The Wall Street Journal* as a "key player in the contact sport of politics."

Today, Scott continues to innovate. He and the Napolitan Institute have partnered with Jigsaw, Google's tech incubator, to develop new ways of measuring public attitudes and values. The results of this "We The People" partnership will be highlighted in events surrounding America's 250th birthday celebration.

Scott focuses on the deeper currents of public opinion and values rather than the surface reaction to passing events. His work consistently shows that the American people continue to embrace our nation's noble founding ideals even if their leaders do not.

His recent work for the Napolitan Institute has shown how the Elite One Percent have rejected those ideals of freedom, equality, and self-governance. His knowledge of history enables him to put events into a larger context and show how this elitist revolt is the root cause of contemporary political turmoil.